William Shakespeare: A Very Short Introduction

VERY SHORT INTRODUCTIONS are for anyone wanting a stimulating and accessible way into a new subject. They are written by experts, and have been translated into more than 40 different languages.

The series began in 1995, and now covers a wide variety of topics in every discipline. The VSI library now contains over 350 volumes—a Very Short Introduction to everything from Psychology and Philosophy of Science to American History and Relativity—and continues to grow in every subject area.

Very Short Introductions available now:

RUSSIAN LITERATURE Catriona Kelly
THE RUSSIAN REVOLUTION
   S. A. Smith
SCHIZOPHRENIA Chris Frith
   and Eve Johnstone
SCHOPENHAUER Christopher Janaway
SCIENCE AND RELIGION
   Thomas Dixon
SCIENCE FICTION David Seed
THE SCIENTIFIC REVOLUTION
   Lawrence M. Principe
SCOTLAND Rab Houston
SEXUALITY Véronique Mottier
SIKHISM Eleanor Nesbitt
THE SILK ROAD James A. Millward
SLEEP Steven W. Lockley
   and Russell G. Foster
SOCIAL AND CULTURAL
   ANTHROPOLOGY
   John Monaghan and Peter Just
SOCIALISM Michael Newman
SOCIOLINGUISTICS John Edwards
SOCIOLOGY Steve Bruce
SOCRATES C. C. W. Taylor
THE SOVIET UNION Stephen Lovell
THE SPANISH CIVIL WAR
   Helen Graham
SPANISH LITERATURE Jo Labanyi
SPINOZA Roger Scruton
SPIRITUALITY Philip Sheldrake
SPORT Mike Cronin
STARS Andrew King
STATISTICS David J. Hand
STEM CELLS Jonathan Slack
STRUCTURAL ENGINEERING
   David Blockley
STUART BRITAIN John Morrill

SUPERCONDUCTIVITY
   Stephen Blundell
SYMMETRY Ian Stewart
TAXATION Stephen Smith
TEETH Peter S. Ungar
TERRORISM Charles Townshend
THEATRE Marvin Carlson
THEOLOGY David F. Ford
THOMAS AQUINAS Fergus Kerr
THOUGHT Tim Bayne
TIBETAN BUDDHISM
   Matthew T. Kapstein
TOCQUEVILLE Harvey C. Mansfield
TRAGEDY Adrian Poole
THE TROJAN WAR Eric H. Cline
TRUST Katherine Hawley
THE TUDORS John Guy
TWENTIETH-CENTURY BRITAIN
   Kenneth O. Morgan
THE UNITED NATIONS
   Jussi M. Hanhimäki
THE U.S. CONGRESS Donald A. Ritchie
THE U.S. SUPREME COURT
   Linda Greenhouse
UTOPIANISM Lyman Tower Sargent
THE VIKINGS Julian Richards
VIRUSES Dorothy H. Crawford
WILLIAM SHAKESPEARE Stanley Wells
WITCHCRAFT Malcolm Gaskill
WITTGENSTEIN A. C. Grayling
WORK Stephen Fineman
WORLD MUSIC Philip Bohlman
THE WORLD TRADE
   ORGANIZATION Amrita Narlikar
WORLD WAR II Gerhard L. Weinberg
WRITING AND SCRIPT
   Andrew Robinson

Available soon:

LIBERALISM Michael Freeden
INFECTIOUS DISEASE
   Marta L. Wayne and
   Benjamin M. Bolker

SOCIAL WORK Sally Holland
   and Jonathan Scourfield
FORESTS Jaboury Ghazoul
PSYCHOANALYSIS Daniel Pick

For more information visit our website

www.oup.com/vsi/

Stanley Wells

WILLIAM SHAKESPEARE

A Very Short Introduction

OXFORD
UNIVERSITY PRESS

OXFORD
UNIVERSITY PRESS

Great Clarendon Street, Oxford, OX2 6DP,
United Kingdom

Oxford University Press is a department of the University of Oxford.
It furthers the University's objective of excellence in research, scholarship,
and education by publishing worldwide. Oxford is a registered trade mark of
Oxford University Press in the UK and in certain other countries

Published in the United States of America by Oxford University Press
198 Madison Avenue, New York, NY 10016, United States of America

British Library Cataloguing in Publication Data

Data available

Library of Congress Control Number: 2014957190

ISBN 978–0–19–871862–8

Printed and bound by CPI Group (UK) Ltd, Croydon, CR0 4YY

Contents

The Cobbe portrait. Advanced on the basis of provenance as Shakespeare in 2005; previously supposed to represent Sir Thomas Overbury.

Preface: Why Shakespeare?

Most people of any education, wherever they may be, have at least heard of Shakespeare. They may know that he was an English poet and playwright who lived quite a long time ago but is famous today. They are likely to be aware that children often learn about him in school. They probably remember the titles of some of his plays—*Romeo and Juliet* and *Hamlet*, at least; perhaps *A Midsummer Night's Dream* and *Macbeth*. They may know a few phrases from them—'To be or not to be', 'Romeo, Romeo, wherefore art thou Romeo?', 'I am a man more sinned against than sinning', 'Once more unto the breach, dear friends'—even if they are a bit hazy about which play they come from or whether perhaps it was someone else who wrote them. Possibly they have visited the Tudor house known as Shakespeare's Birthplace in Stratford-upon-Avon; they may have come across a rumour that he was an impostor and that someone else, probably an aristocrat, wrote his plays for him.

Some people may have had to learn speeches from Shakespeare plays by heart—perhaps one starting 'The quality of mercy is not strained', or 'Is this a dagger which I see before me?', or a sonnet such as 'Shall I compare thee to a summer's day?' Such a task may have been imposed on them as a punishment. They may have had to take part in a classroom reading, or to act in a scene from one of the plays in front of their schoolfellows. Possibly at a wedding or a civil partnership ceremony they have heard someone read the sonnet that begins 'Let me not to the marriage of true minds admit impediments'. Perhaps they have been taken to see one of the plays performed by amateurs, or by a professional company, or on film, and have enjoyed it more than they expected. On the other hand they may have sat through it in mystified boredom while longing to get to the pub before closing time.

As they got older such people may have become scientists or lawyers or artisans or businessmen or nurses or shop assistants and have felt that Shakespeare was at most a thing of their past, just something you had to 'do' at school and now read about from time to time in the newspapers or switched off when it came up on the television.

But then something may have happened to stir their interest. They may have gone to see a Shakespeare play or film to keep someone else company or because a famous film or television star—a Helen Mirren or a Kevin Spacey—was acting in it, and have been surprised to find that they understood and even enjoyed it more than they expected. They may have got to know someone for whom Shakespeare was a passion. Perhaps they have felt a bit out of things because a form of entertainment that clearly means a lot to other people was a closed book to them. They may even have been a bit abashed by reading that a character in Jane Austen's novel *Mansfield Park* said: 'Shakespeare one gets acquainted with without knowing how. It is a part of an Englishman's constitution. His thoughts and beauties are so spread abroad that one touches them everywhere; one is intimate with him by instinct. No man of any brain can open at a good part of one of his plays without falling into the flow of his meaning immediately.' Their interest may have been sparked enough for them to want to know more.

These are the kinds of people for whom this book is written. They could lead happy and useful lives without Shakespeare, just as they could also sail through life in ignorance of quantum physics, or Buddhism, or Greek tragedy, or Nōh drama, or *Dr Who*, or *Strictly Come Dancing*, or The Rolling Stones. No one has a moral duty to like Shakespeare. On the other hand there are many good reasons why it is worth allowing him into your life. To ignore his work suggests an indifference to a major source of intellectual and spiritual enrichment. And it limits one's response to many other areas of human experience.

I hope, in this short book about the man and his writings, to persuade readers who were previously indifferent to Shakespeare that it is worth getting to know more about him, to try to understand what it is about his plays and poems that causes them to mean so much to so many people—in short, to discover what all the fuss is about.

List of illustrations

Chapter 1
Shakespeare and
Stratford-upon-Avon

First, his life. Shakespeare was born and grew up in a small but generally prosperous market town in the English Midlands. The parish register of Stratford-upon-Avon records the baptism on Wednesday 26 April 1564 in Holy Trinity Church of 'Gulielmus, filius Johannes Shakspere'—William, son of John Shakespeare. It is written in Latin because this was the language used in official documents at that time. There was no legal process of registering births. Many babies died soon after they were born, so it was customary to baptize them, as the Prayer Book recommended, 'no later than the Sunday or other holy day next after the child be born'. Sunday would have been the 23rd, and the monument in Holy Trinity says that Shakespeare was 53 when he died on 23 April 1616, which must mean that he had started his fifty-third year—that is, he had been born on or before 23 April 1564. Since the 18th century Shakespeare's birthday has, reasonably enough, been celebrated on 23 April.

William's father, John, was in his mid-thirties in 1564. He came of farming stock and had lived as a boy in the village of Snitterfield, about three miles north of Stratford. He had probably moved to the town as a young man to learn the trade of whitawer—a tanner of white leather—and glover, which required an apprenticeship of at least seven years. He developed other business interests, too, including, logically enough, wool-dealing. His wife Mary, whose maiden name was Arden, came from a rather more prosperous background and seems to have been a woman of practical ability, since her father chose her above her seven sisters, two stepsisters, and two stepbrothers as his executor and left her the bulk of his estate. The house in which she lived before she married, now known, along with adjoining property, as Mary Arden's Farm, is in Wilmcote, also about three miles to the north of Stratford but to the west of Snitterfield.

After they married John and Mary lived in the house in Henley Street, Stratford-upon-Avon, now known as Shakespeare's Birthplace. It's a substantial dwelling—bigger, indeed, than many ordinary houses today (admittedly people tended to have more children then than now). Two daughters died in infancy before William came along, and John and Mary went on to have three more sons and two more daughters, all of whom survived into adulthood. Gilbert, born in 1566, died in 1612 and appears to have been a haberdasher and to have lived for a time in London, but he signed a document on behalf of his brother William, who must have been out of town, concerning the purchase of land in Stratford-upon-Avon in 1602 and was buried there in 1612.

The other Shakespeare brothers also made little mark on the records. All we know of Richard is his dates of birth and death: 11 March 1574 and 4 February 1613. Neither Gilbert nor he appears to have married. The youngest, Edmund, was William's junior by sixteen years; he, too, became an actor in London, but little is known about him except that he died in 1607 aged only 27, five weeks after the death in infancy of his illegitimate son. His big brother William probably paid for his funeral, which is recorded as taking place on 31 December during a great frost in what is now Southwark Cathedral, close to the Globe playhouse, with, exceptionally and expensively, a tolling of the great bell. Of his sisters, Anne, baptized in 1571, died when she was only 7 years old; her parents paid a special fee for the tolling of the church bell and a pall carried or spread over her coffin. The longest lived of all was Joan, born in 1569, who married a hatter, William Hart, by whom she had four children. Shakespeare left her the house that had belonged to their parents—the Birthplace; she died in 1646 but the house remained in the family's possession until 1806.

Shakespeare's father John was a successful businessman who came to play a major part in civic life, becoming an alderman and rising to the exalted rank of bailiff (or mayor) in 1568. Like many able men and women at that time, he signed documents with a mark and may not have been able to write, but he could not have carried out his civic duties without being able to read. He was born before the Reformation; late and unreliable evidence suggests that he may have retained Roman Catholic sympathies, but churchgoing was required by law and during his period of office as bailiff he, wearing the robes and insignia of his office, along with his family would have been escorted to their seats in Holy Trinity by civic officials each Sunday. Both at church and at home Shakespeare would have gained the familiarity with the Bible, the Book of Common Prayer, and the Homilies that is apparent from his writings. All the evidence suggests that he and his family subscribed to the doctrines of the established Church of England.

Stratford was—as it still is—a market town situated on the picturesque river Avon in the famously well-wooded and leafy county of Warwickshire. Here Shakespeare would have gained the familiarity with countryside pursuits and sports which is apparent in his writings—hunting, fishing, falconry, swimming among them. The town had a horse fair; Shakespeare would probably have learned to ride at an early age; two of his sonnets (50 and 51) are written, as it were, on horseback. Trees, especially elms, abounded. A pub called the One Elm now marks what was once the north-westerly boundary.

Though the town has grown outwards over the centuries the layout of its core is still as it was in Shakespeare's time, and many houses, inns, and other buildings of the period survive, in various states of preservation. It had up to 2,000 inhabitants, many of whom, along with men and women from the neighbouring villages, would have bought and sold their wares in the market place on the appointed days. The splendid parish church still stands on the outskirts; its spire is an 18th century addition.

In the town centre is the smaller chapel which served the members of the numerous guilds, or trading companies, into which the town's workers were organized. Its interior walls had been painted with biblical scenes before the Reformation but during John Shakespeare's term of office as bailiff he was required to ensure that their Popish images were whitewashed over. Now they are partially restored. Next to the chapel, on Church Street, stands the long two-storeyed building which housed the grammar school on one floor and the guildhall on the other. Beyond those, on the way out of town and towards the church, are the ancient almshouses, still used as housing for elderly townspeople.

We know quite a lot about Shakespeare's Stratford because records of the town were kept in a large wooden chest which survives. They have been meticulously edited, and help us to form a detailed picture of life during Shakespeare's boyhood and lifetime. The town had more than its fair share of disasters. Less than three months after Shakespeare was born, plague struck. 'Hic incepit pestis'—the plague started here—reads a terse entry in the parish register. Within six months, close on 240 townspeople died, including four children of a single family close to the Shakespeares' house, in Henley Street. Members of the Town Council discussed ways of providing financial help to families that had suffered, the grammar school closed, and some mothers fled with their children for safety to relatives in the countryside.

Fire was a special hazard in a town where almost all the buildings were made of wood, many of them thatched with straw, and the town suffered several major conflagrations during Shakespeare's lifetime. In 1594 one of the houses destroyed belonged to the bailiff, Thomas Rogers, whose daughter Katharine was to give birth in 1608 to John Harvard, founder of Harvard University. Splendidly restored in 1595 with superb wood carving, it is known as Harvard House. Another fire destroyed around 200 homes and other buildings in the following year, and yet another ravaged the town in 1614. Disasters such as these imposed heavy burdens on the town's officials. One of these who sought for relief both among their fellow townsmen and further afield was Richard Quiney, a frequent visitor on town affairs to London.

Among the papers found in the town chest is a petition of 1604 on behalf of a man called Thomas Parker which shows that education was available even for quite small children, girls as well as boys; he 'employed himself to the teaching of little children, chiefly such as his wife one time of the day doth practise in needlework, whereby our young youth is well furthered in reading and the free school greatly eased of that tedious trouble'. The 'free school' is the town's grammar school, one of many founded—or in this case re-founded—by King Edward VI in 1553. All its pupils were boys. It is still there and started to admit girls only in 2013. Men who taught at the school in Shakespeare's time were Oxford graduates, and some Stratford boys went on to study at Oxford University.

Such schools provided a rigorous education, primarily in oratory, rhetoric, and classical literature, comparable in some areas to that of university graduates in Classics of the present day. From an early age the boys were required both to write and to speak in Latin. A letter written in Latin by Richard Quiney's son aged about 11 when he was presumably a pupil at the grammar school asks his father to bring back from London books of blank paper for himself and his brother, and expresses gratitude for being brought up in 'the studies of sacred learning'—'educasti me in sacrae doctrinae studiis usque ad hunc diem.' A scene (4.1) in *The Merry Wives of Windsor* in which a boy called William is put through his paces in Latin grammar and in which Shakespeare quotes from a textbook prescribed for use in every such school in the kingdom is surely the most autobiographical in all the plays.

We have no documentary evidence that William—or anyone else—attended the school, because no records of pupils survive before 1800. On the other hand, it has been exhaustively shown in a great two-volume work by T. W. Baldwin called *Shakspere's Smalle Latine and Less Greeke*—the title is a quotation from Ben Jonson's tribute to Shakespeare, printed in the First Folio of 1623—that the grammar-school curriculum of the time would have provided all the classical knowledge necessary to write the plays and poems of William Shakespeare.

Shakespeare's education

Here Shakespeare would have read some of the great works of classical literature that would feed his imagination and provide raw material for his poems and plays throughout his career. Roman comedies which introduced him to the principles of dramatic craftsmanship would have been on the syllabus: one of them, *Menaechmi*, by Plautus, was to give him the plot for *The Comedy of Errors*. Ovid's great poem *Metamorphoses*, which tells many myths and legends of the ancient world, was clearly one of Shakespeare's favourite books. An episode from it forms the basis of his long narrative poem *Venus and Adonis*, of 1593, he alludes to or quotes from it in many plays, bringing it on stage in both *Titus Andronicus* and *Cymbeline*, and in *The Tempest* one of Prospero's greatest speeches, the one beginning 'Ye elves of hills, brooks, standing lakes' (5.1.33–57), is virtually a translation of lines from it.

He would have been able to see and even to take part in plays in Stratford, too. Touring professional companies regularly included the town in their itineraries during his boyhood and youth, and local amateurs put on entertainments, especially at Whitsuntide. In 1583, when Shakespeare was 19, the Town Council subsidized an entertainment by one Davy Jones—who, like Shakespeare, married a member of the Hathaway family—and his company, which could have included Shakespeare.

A fellow Stratfordian, Richard Field, three years older than Shakespeare, went on to become a distinguished London printer and publisher of learned books written in several languages. He printed three of Shakespeare's non-dramatic works—the poems *Venus and Adonis* (1593), *The Rape of Lucrece* (1594), and 'The Phoenix and the Turtle' (part of a larger collection) in 1601; and in *Cymbeline*, written towards the end of Shakespeare's career, there is a pun on Field's name when the heroine, Innogen, says that the headless corpse which she believes to be her husband's body (it's that kind of play) is that of 'Richard Duchamp'—'Richard of the field'. It is virtually certain that the two were lifelong friends.

Shakespeare had probably left school when he was about 15, but he didn't leave Stratford immediately. We don't know what he did for a living at first. He may have helped in his father's business. He may have been kept on at the school as an 'usher'—an assistant master—to teach the younger boys: late in the 17th century the gossipy diarist John Aubrey wrote that in his youth Shakespeare had been 'a schoolmaster in the country', where 'country' may have referred to Stratford.

He was an early developer sexually. At this time most men in the town married when they were between 20 and 30, and on average at the age of 24. Shakespeare was only 18 when, towards the end of 1582, he married Anne Hathaway, from nearby Shottery. She was 26. A daughter, Susanna, was baptized six months later, indicating that Shakespeare and Anne had committed what was then the crime of premarital fornication. In *Measure for Measure* a young man, Claudio, narrowly escapes execution for the same offence. Shakespeare had better luck. Twins, Hamnet and Judith, were baptized on 2 February 1585.

By this time Shakespeare must have been aware that, however strong the pull of family life, his future lay away from Stratford, in the literary and theatrical world that centred on London. Except for a passing mention in a law case of 1587, there's a gap in the record after the birth of the twins until 1592. This period is often called the 'lost years'. Innumerable guesses have been made about what he was doing. It has been suggested that he worked in a lawyer's office, that he became a soldier or a sailor, and so on. But he must have started his career as a man of the theatre reasonably early during this period. Perhaps the best guess is that at some point he joined a theatre company—maybe even one of those that visited Stratford—whether as actor or writer or both. And before long he was writing plays, sometimes (as was common) in collaboration with others. His wife and children appear to have stayed in Stratford. Tragically, his only son Hamnet died and was buried there in August 1596; his grave is unknown and there is no telling whether Shakespeare was able to be present for his son's burial.

Shakespeare was deeply committed to the town of his birth throughout his life. In May 1597 he had become wealthy enough to buy New Place (Figure 1), the second biggest house in Stratford-upon-Avon—only the stone-built College, close to the church, was larger. Presumably, in buying New Place, Shakespeare was deliberately making provision not only for himself and his family, but also for his parents and perhaps for other relatives. Servants would have been needed to help to run it. In London he lived only in a series of modest lodgings, a fact which increases the likelihood that he regarded Stratford-upon-Avon as his real home, even though it would have taken two or three days to get there on horseback. He was the first great literary commuter. Theatres were closed during

1. New Place: an artist's impression.

Lent, which might have given him more opportunity than usual to ride home, perhaps to write in (relative) peace, as well as to see his family.

Shakespeare's growing social aspirations, witnessed by his purchase of a house much larger than he and his immediate family needed, are reflected also in the application made in 1596 (ostensibly by his father, but probably by William acting on his father's behalf) to the College of Heralds for a coat of arms, which would bestow on him and his descendants the status of gentleman and the right to be termed 'Master'. The seal and crest are displayed on Shakespeare's monument and on his daughter Susanna's seal.

He kept up his involvement with the town's affairs. The only surviving letter addressed to him is a request written on 15 October 1598 by Richard Quiney, who was on a visit to London on civic business, asking for security for a loan of the large sum of £30, probably on behalf of the town rather than for himself. Quiney must have thought of Shakespeare as a wealthy man. The letter was found among Quiney's papers, which suggests that it was never delivered; maybe Quiney was able to speak to Shakespeare in person.

Shakespeare's father John died in 1601, apparently leaving no will. As the eldest son Shakespeare would have inherited the Henley Street house in which his mother continued to live. He may also have inherited money: in 1602 he consolidated his possessions by spending the great sum of £320 for the purchase of 107 acres of land in Old Stratford. This may have been intended as a marriage settlement for his elder daughter Susanna. In the same year he bought a cottage with a decent-sized garden in College Lane, close to New Place, probably for the use of a servant. In 1605 he was wealthy enough to pay £440 for an interest in the Stratford tithes. A major investment, it would have brought him an annual income of around £40—twice the salary of the local vicar.

In 1607 Susanna married the physician John Hall; their only child, Elizabeth, was born a barely respectable nine months later. She married twice and, Shakespeare's last descendant, died, prosperous but childless, in 1670. In London in March 1613 Shakespeare made yet another substantial investment, paying £140 for the Blackfriars gatehouse. The deed of purchase describes him as of Stratford-upon-Avon; this was probably an investment pure and simple.

Also in March 1613 Shakespeare was paid 44 shillings in gold for composing an impresa—a kind of motto—for the Earl of Rutland to display in a tilt, or tournament, on the King's Accession Day. His friend and colleague Richard Burbage, an artist as well as a great actor, designed it. The last two or three plays in which Shakespeare had a hand were written in collaboration with John Fletcher; *Henry VIII*, or *All Is True*, as it was known at the time, was being performed at the Globe on 29 June 1613 when the firing of a cannon set the thatch on fire, burning the playhouse to the ground. *The Two Noble Kinsmen* seems to have been written a little later, and there is reason to believe that Shakespeare and Fletcher also wrote together a play, now lost, called *Cardenio*, which to judge from its title was based on an episode from *Don Quixote*. Nothing later has survived, but Shakespeare remained active in Stratford affairs and continued to invest money. Late in 1614 he was implicated in negotiations relating to the enclosure of land in his home town, including some that he owned, changing its use from arable to sheep pasture, a move which would have brought further poverty to the town's poorer inhabitants.

In January 1616, probably knowing that he had not long to live, Shakespeare summoned his lawyer to draw up a will, which survives only in the form of a draft revised a couple of months later. It is easy to see why he made changes. His second daughter Judith, now 31, married Richard Quiney's son Thomas, a vintner, on 10 February. Within weeks a scandal erupted involving the groom. It turned out that Thomas had been carrying on an affair with a woman, Margaret Wheeler, who had borne him a son; mother and child died of unknown causes on 15 March. Eleven days later, only six weeks after marrying Judith, Thomas was prosecuted for the crime of sexual incontinency and sentenced to perform penance on three successive Sundays wearing a white sheet betokening humility before the entire Stratford congregation. Perhaps because someone—possibly his father-in-law—intervened on his behalf, Thomas escaped with a fine of five shillings instead, paid to the poor of the parish, and with a less humiliating formal confession, wearing his normal clothes, before the minister of the smaller, neighbouring parish of Bishopton.

Shakespeare's revisions to his will make changes designed to safeguard Judith's interests in case her marriage failed. She receives £150 and the interest on a further £150 if she is still alive and married three years later, as well as a silver-gilt bowl (could it still be in existence somewhere?). His granddaughter Elizabeth gets the rest of his plate. The bulk of Shakespeare's property goes to his eldest daughter, Susanna. His sister gets the Henley Street house and his clothes (probably a valuable bequest). There are other bequests to his sister Joan's three sons, to his godson, to the poor of Stratford (£10), and to friends and neighbours. He leaves 26s. and 8d. to three colleagues in the King's Men—Richard Burbage, Henry Condell, and John Heminges—to buy mourning rings—a common practice. His sword, symbol of his status as a gentleman and a King's Man, went to Thomas Coombe, a 27-year-old lawyer, member of a prominent and wealthy Stratford family with whom Shakespeare had close links.

The most mysterious aspect of Shakespeare's will is the now famous bequest to his wife of nothing more than his 'second-best bed'. There has been endless speculation about whether this is an insult or a compliment—it could have been the matrimonial bed—and whether he knew that she would in any case be well provided for. Odd it certainly seems and I have no explanation to offer. We know, however, that Anne Shakespeare continued to live at New Place, presumably cared for by her daughter.

As I have said, Shakespeare died on 23 April 1616 and was buried in Holy Trinity. He was just 53. We don't know the cause of his death. A monument set up in the chancel of Holy Trinity offers a disappointingly stolid image along with an inscription in Latin comparing him to great figures of antiquity and another in English praising him as a great writer (Figure 2). The gravestone traditionally identified as his is inscribed only with the epitaph:

> Good friend for Jesus sake forbeare,
> To dig the dust enclosed here.
> Blessed be the man that spares these stones,
> And cursed be he that moves my bones.

2. The monument in Holy Trinity Church, Stratford-upon-Avon.

It is written in the first person, which may—or may not—mean that Shakespeare is the author.

Shakespeare's reading

So far as we know Shakespeare was the only member of his family to have had artistic leanings or literary aspirations, and to have developed poetic ambitions early in life. He probably read widely outside the school curriculum even as a young man, and he would have had to write both prose and verse at school. One of his less distinguished sonnets—irregular in that it is written in octosyllabic iambic metre instead of the usual ten-syllabled lines—is a gently, ruefully humorous love poem which seems to report a rapidly resolved lovers' quarrel:

> Those lips that Love's [i.e. Cupid's] own hand did make
> Breathed forth the sound that said 'I hate,'
> To me that languished for her sake:
> But when she saw my woeful state,
> Straight in her heart did mercy come,
> Chiding that tongue that ever sweet
> Was used in giving gentle doom,
> And taught it thus anew to greet:
> 'I hate' she altered with an end,
> That followed it as gentle day
> Doth follow night, who like a fiend
> From heaven to hell is flown away;
> > 'I hate' from hate away she threw,
> > And saved my life, saying—'not you.'
>
> (Sonnet 145)

The awkwardly phrased last two lines are easily explained as a pun on the name 'Hathaway.' Even 'And' in the next line recalls 'Anne.'

This sonnet, written presumably around 1582, before Shakespeare married, could easily be his first surviving composition, preserved among his papers, perhaps for sentimental reasons, until a collection of his sonnets got into print in 1609. It links him curiously with a character in one of his own plays. In *The Merry Wives of Windsor* the foolish young Abraham Slender, seeking inspiration in his desire to woo another Anne—Anne Page—says, 'I had rather than forty shillings I had my book of songs and sonnets here' (1.1.181–2). He is speaking of a popular book, *Songs and Sonnets Written by the Right Honourable Lord Henry Howard, late Earl of Surrey, Thomas Wyatt the Elder and others*, commonly known as *Tottel's Miscellany*, first published in 1557 and frequently reprinted. No doubt Shakespeare owned a copy. The sonnet form was to be extremely important for him, not only in the 154 poems published in 1609 but in his plays too, especially the early comedies, which have sonnets embedded in their dialogue, and in *Romeo and Juliet*, which opens with a prologue in sonnet form, in which the chorus to Act 2 also has this form, and in which the lovers speak a shared sonnet at their first meeting. In later plays, too, sonnet form crops up from time to time, as in the epilogue to *Henry V* (see Chapter 4), in *All's Well That Ends Well* (3.3.4–17), and late in his career in *Cymbeline* (5.5.187–207).

Shakespeare was surely an avid reader of English as well as classical literature from an early age. Both as a writer and as an incipient man of the theatre he was born at the right time. He grew up during a period of increasing national stability and prosperity. Queen Elizabeth was unifying the nation. Especially in the wake of the Spanish Armada of 1588, patriotic sentiment was increasing, witnessed by the number of plays of the 1590s written by Shakespeare and other writers which take English history as their subject matter. The arts in general were flourishing; this is a great age of English music, painting, and architecture. And under the influence partly of humanist interest in classical and Italian civilization, the two or three decades after Shakespeare's birth saw extraordinary developments in many different literary kinds. John Lyly's two-part fiction *Euphues*, which created a sudden, short-lived vogue for a highly ornate prose style, much imitated by many other writers, was published in 1578 and 1580, when Shakespeare was a teenager; he parodies its style in speeches of Falstaff in *Henry IV, Part One* (e.g. 2.5.402–22). One of the greatest and most versatile of literary innovators was the multi-talented soldier and courtier Sir Philip Sidney, who, thwarted by the Queen of his ambitions for a life of action, wrote between about 1579 and 1584 the first great English sonnet sequence, *Astrophil and Stella*; the first great work of English prose fiction, *Arcadia* (around 1580, with an uncompleted revision four years later); and a major work of literary criticism, *The Apologie for Poetry*, which is itself a masterly work of poetic prose. All these books were published during the years following Sidney's heroic and untimely death, in 1587; there are echoes of *Astrophil and Stella* in *Romeo and Juliet*, and Shakespeare was to draw on *Arcadia* for the Gloucester plot of *King Lear*. During this period too Edmund Spenser was writing his long allegorical epic poem *The Faerie Queene*, which started to appear in 1590 and which too is echoed in Shakespeare's plays.

Shakespeare's early years also saw the publication of major historical writings that were to provide him with much plot material. The first volume of Raphael Holinshed's *Chronicles of England, Scotland and Ireland* (actually a multi-authored work), which gave Shakespeare masses of material for his English history plays as well as for *Macbeth* and *King Lear*, was published in 1577, with an expanded edition ten years later. As a boy Shakespeare may even have met Holinshed, who died in 1580 and lived not far from Stratford in later life.

It was a great time for translations, too. The Greek historian Plutarch's *Parallel Lives* of Greek and Roman emperors appeared in 1579 in a fine translation by Sir Thomas North, who worked from a version in French. This book not only gave Shakespeare narrative material for *Julius Caesar*, *Coriolanus*, and *Antony and Cleopatra*, he also found its style so attractive that at times he drew heavily on North's prose, turning it into incandescent poetry as, most famously, in Enobarbus' speech describing Cleopatra in her barge on the river Cydnus—'The barge she sat in like a burnished throne | Burned on the water . . .' (2.2.198–225). Translators also helped to make available to English readers the writings of French and, especially, Italian story tellers such as Giovanni Boccaccio (1313–75) in the *Decameron*, translated partially by William Painter in 1566 when Shakespeare was 2 years old, from which he took plot material for *All's Well That Ends Well* and *Cymbeline*.

During these years, too, many lesser writers were producing books that Shakespeare was to read and to make use of. Arthur Brooke's long poem *Romeus and Juliet* appeared two years before Shakespeare was born; he drew on it heavily for his play about the young lovers. Robert Greene (1558–92), a prolific and versatile man of letters, wrote short books about London's low life known as the coney-catching pamphlets which appeared around 1590, two of the first romantic comedies, *Friar Bacon and Friar Bungay* and *James IV*, and many works of prose fiction, one of which, *Pandosto*, published in 1588, Shakespeare was to turn into a play, *The Winter's Tale*, some twenty years later. Thomas Lodge published his prose romance *Rosalynde* in 1590; Shakespeare dramatized it around 1600 as *As You Like It*; it is intriguing to think that Lodge, who later became a distinguished physician, may have been in the audience at early performances of the play that his book inspired.

Chapter 2
Theatre in Shakespeare's time

Both drama and theatre were developing rapidly in Shakespeare's early years. The first purpose-built playhouse, the Red Lion, went up in London in 1567; it lasted only a few months, but was followed in 1576 by The Theatre, built by James Burbage whose son, Richard, was to become the leading actor of Shakespeare's company; this event inaugurated the greatest period of the English drama, lasting till the closing of the playhouses in 1642.

The first great wave of writers for these stages included those who have come to be known as the University Wits—John Lyly, Thomas Lodge, Christopher Marlowe, George Peele, Thomas Nashe, and Robert Greene, along with Thomas Kyd, author of *The Spanish Tragedy*, who is not known to have been a university man. Shakespeare followed rapidly in their footsteps, learning from them, even collaborating with and imitating some of them. Especially in his early days in London, whether working as writer or as actor, he must have seen many plays, absorbing influences from those that he saw on stage, acted in, and read. Within the month of January 1593 alone, we know from the papers of the theatre financier Philip Henslowe, playgoers at the Rose were offered performances of *Titus Andronicus*, in which Shakespeare had collaborated with Peele, *Harry the Sixth* (presumably *Henry VI, Part One,* currently believed to have been written by Shakespeare with Thomas Nashe), Marlowe's *The Jew of Malta* and *The Massacre at Paris*, Thomas Kyd's *The Spanish Tragedy*, *Friar Bacon and Friar Bungay* by Robert Greene, who had recently died, and several other plays, some of which have not survived. The highest receipts were for the plays by Marlowe. During this month, at least, Shakespeare and Marlowe must have spent time together in the playhouse where they were having such success.

Marlowe was not an actor, but Shakespeare was; his name appears, for example, in the cast lists of plays by Jonson and heads the list of actors printed in the First Folio of his own plays. He may well have appeared in some of the plays given at the Rose. Marlowe's 'mighty line', as Ben Jonson was later to characterize his verse, influenced Shakespeare, as did his more lyrical poetry. In his *Dr Faustus*, Faustus' address to Helen of Troy, 'Was this the face that launched a thousand ships?', finds echoes in several Shakespeare plays, most notably in *Troilus and Cressida*—'Why, she is a pearl | Whose price has launched above a thousand ships ...' (2.2.80–1), written before Marlowe's play had appeared in print. Kyd's powerful rhetoric finds echoes in, especially, Shakespeare's early histories and in *Titus Andronicus*. Greene's romantic comedies *James IV* (not a history play, in spite of its title) and *Friar Bacon and Friar Bungay* have a lyric charm that pre-echoes some of Shakespeare's romantic comedies. And the wit and charm of Lyly's elegant comedies, written from 1584 onwards to be played by boys' companies, taught Shakespeare much about the composition of comic dialogue in plays such as *The Two Gentlemen of Verona* and *Love's Labour's Lost*.

It is, or seems to be, Robert Greene who gives us the first, cryptic indication that Shakespeare has arrived on the London literary scene. In a book of 1592 called *Greene's Groatsworth of Wit* (now believed to have been ghost-written by its publisher, Henry Chettle), the writer says, 'there is an upstart crow, beautified with our feathers, that with his *tiger's heart wrapped in a player's hide* supposes he is as well able to bombast out a blank verse as the best of you; and, being an absolute *Johannes Factotum*, is in his own conceit the only Shake-scene in a country.'

'Shake-scene' clearly puns on the name 'Shakespeare', and 'tiger's heart wrapped in a player's hide' paraphrases a line from one of the most memorable scenes in Shakespeare's *The True Tragedy of Richard, Duke of York*, later known as *Henry VI, Part Three*: 'O tiger's heart wrapped in a woman's hide!' (1.4.138). In 'beautified with our feathers' the writer claims to be speaking on behalf of fellow playwrights, as well as himself, in resentment at the success of an actor turned playwright, whom he may also be accusing of plagiarism. The allusion is uncomplimentary; but clearly Shakespeare had arrived.

The theatrical scene

The reference in *Greene's Groatsworth of Wit* suggests that Shakespeare was already well established on the London theatrical scene by 1592. The profession was strictly regulated by government control. As early as 1559, before England had any permanent theatre buildings, a proclamation decreed that no plays treating of 'matters of religion or the governance of the estate of the commonwealth' should be performed; this had a profound and long-lasting effect on the content of plays, inhibiting dramatists from direct treatment of religious or political matters. Needless to say, some writers managed to express their views indirectly, but the government attempted to enforce its regulations by censorship; in 1581 it decreed that all plays should be given a trial run before the Master of the Revels, Edmund Tilney, before being offered to the public. Tilney and his department had heavy responsibilities relating to the practicalities of performance of plays at court. He held the office until 1610; he and his successors censored written scripts as well as seeing trial performances based on them.

The subject matter of some plays was politically sensitive even if it did not relate directly to current events. In the late years of

Elizabeth's reign the question of who would succeed her on the throne became a highly sensitive topic; apparently as a result, the episode in Shakespeare's *Richard II* showing the deposition of the King was omitted when the play was first printed, in 1597, and presumably when it was staged; it was restored to the printed text after the issue had been resolved by the accession of James I in 1603.

Language could be censored too. An 'Act to Restrain Abuses of Players' of 1606 instituted a fine of the large sum of £10 for each time an actor 'jestingly or profanely' spoke the name of God or Jesus Christ. Cunningly, half the fine went to any member of the public who reported the offence. The effects of this law can be seen in the texts of some Shakespeare plays. The version of *Othello* printed in 1622, which seems to be based on the play as Shakespeare first wrote it, around 1603–4, has over fifty oaths that are toned down in the more theatrical text printed in the First Folio of 1623.

The social status of actors was also a matter of government concern and control. It is not true, as is sometimes said, that all actors were classed as rogues and vagabonds; this label applied only to entertainers of many different kinds, such as jugglers, tightrope walkers, those involved in bear baiting, cock and dog fighting, as well as itinerant actors, if they were not members of an organized company that had the patronage of a nobleman, or even of the Queen herself. Other actors, including Shakespeare and many of his colleagues, became prosperous and highly respected members of society. Some noblemen employed companies of actors as full-time members of their households; others conferred more or less nominal patronage on playing companies whose members acted under their banner.

In 1583 the Queen awarded her patronage to a troupe cherry-picked from other companies who played initially in London, then from 1594 on tour in the English counties. This troupe, the Queen's Men, visited Stratford in the summer of 1587, a couple of years after the birth of Shakespeare's twins. One of the actors had recently been killed in a brawl in nearby Thame, in Oxfordshire, and it has been conjectured that Shakespeare took his place, though the idea that the country's top acting company would wish to employ a young man of no professional experience as either actor or writer, however promising he might be, seems far-fetched. Nevertheless, there is good reason to believe that he was associated with this company early in his career; their repertory included four plays—*The Famous Victories of Henry the Fifth*, *The Troublesome Reign of King John*, *The True Tragedy of Richard the Third*, and *King Leir*—on topics that he was to take up later.

Playing spaces

In London before purpose-built playing houses went up, and on tour, companies played in improvised places—royal palaces for court performances, the halls of great houses, courtyards of inns, guildhalls such as Stratford's, town halls, even sometimes in churches. The system must often have required last-minute adjustment to the texts of the plays they were giving if, for example, there was no trap to serve as Ophelia's grave, or no upper level for Juliet's window.

The building of the Theatre in 1576 was a momentous event, and one which heralded the golden age of English theatre and drama. The playhouse was located in Shoreditch, well north of the walls surrounding the City of London, whose authorities frowned on dramatic performances. This was partly because the Puritans among them regarded playhouses, in which boys impersonated women, where serious matters might be lightly treated, and where comedy was often lewd, as dens of vice. A number of sermons written soon after the Theatre went up inveigh intemperately against playacting. One Philip Stubbes, for example, wrote in 1583 that 'these goodly pageants being ended, every mate sorts to his mate, everyone brings another homeward of their way very friendly, and in their secret conclaves they play the sodomites or worse' ('sodomites' could refer to any kinds of sexual transgressors).

More reasonably, the authorities feared that large assemblies of people would attract thieves and prostitutes and spread infection in time of plague. This made them permit playhouses to be built only outside the City limits, in what were known as the liberties. Mostly they went up on the south bank of the Thames, in the parish of Southwark. There from 1587 stood the Rose, the only one of which substantial remains have so far been excavated, from 1595 the Swan, which gives us the only drawing of a theatre interior of the period (Figure 3), and from 1599 the Globe, close to the Rose. In this area too there were many inns, bull- and bear-baiting rings—some of which doubled as playhouses—and brothels.

The design of theatres did much to influence the nature of the plays written to be performed in them. It was not uniform, and it evolved over time, but typically public playhouses were three storeys high, circular or many-sided, and open to the air, with a stage jutting out from the lowest gallery into the yard. Audiences would pay one penny for standing room in front of the stage. These were what Hamlet calls the groundlings. As the word originally meant a small fish that lived in mud at the bottom of a stream or river, the term is not a compliment. If patrons wanted a seat in one of the ranks of galleries that surrounded the yard they paid another penny. There was also what was known as the Lords' Room, close to the stage, where more privileged playgoers sat, as well as space for musicians.

The stage itself would have a trap door, and a roof, or canopy, which might be supported by pillars. It could hold flying equipment for the descent of Jupiter in *Cymbeline* or of the goddesses in *The Tempest*. At the back would be two doorways, left

The labels in the drawing read: *tectum*, *porticus*, *sedilia*, *orchestra*, *ingressus*, *mimorum aedes*, *proscaenium*, *planities sive arena*.

Ex observationibus Londinensibus Johannis de Witt

3. The Swan Theatre: a copy made after 1596–7 of a drawing by Arendt van Buchell of a sketch by Johannes de Witt.

and right, from which actors could come and go, and a broader central aperture which might be used for mass entries and for properties such as Desdemona's bed, in *Othello*, and where Polonius could hide before being stabbed, in *Hamlet*. Above this was an upper level, where Juliet could appear—'But soft, what light from yonder window breaks?', says Romeo—and to which Antony would be hauled for his death scene in *Antony and Cleopatra*. There were stairs so that actors could reach the upper level from the main stage. Behind the stage would be the tiring ('attiring') house, where costumes and properties would be kept and actors would dress. And high up, on the third level of the Globe, at least, there was a hut from which a trumpeter would signal that a performance was imminent, and above that a flag flew to signal that the play was in progress.

There was no scenery in the modern sense of the word, but costumes and properties could be elaborate. The most detailed records of an Elizabethan theatre company that survive are for the Lord Admiral's Men, which performed at the Rose, with Edward Alleyn as their leading actor; they were the chief rivals of the company to which Shakespeare was to belong for most of his career. Inventories that this company made in 1598 include, besides many different kinds of costumes, such picturesque items as 'the Moor's limbs, and Hercules' limbs', 'four Turks' heads', 'one fool's coat, cape and bauble', and a list of instruments which illustrates how important a part music, sadly little of which survives, could play in these theatres: '3 trumpets and a drum, and a treble viol, and a bass viol, a bandore, a cittern.' There were also substantial scenic properties such as '1 rock, 1 tomb, 1 hell mouth, 1 golden fleece, 2 racket, 1 bay tree', 'the cloth of the sun and moon', '2 moss banks', '2 coffins', '1 dragon in *Faustus*' (Marlowe's *Dr Faustus*, performed by this company), 'the City of Rome' (whatever that may be—possibly a painted cloth) and '1 cauldron for the Jew' (another play by Marlowe, *The Jew of Malta*, at the end of which the Jew drops into a cauldron of boiling oil).

The easiest way for a modern playgoer in England to gain a sense of what playhouses of the time were like is to visit Shakespeare's Globe on Bankside, a modern reconstruction set up not far from the site of its Elizabethan counterpart. Since no plans for that survive, some aspects of the modern building, including its overall size, are conjectural, and it makes use of artificial lighting, but many of its features are historically accurate.

The actors

The actors who played in these theatres were organized into companies, always under high-ranking patronage. All were male—women actors played no part in the professional theatre in England until after the restoration of the monarchy, in 1660. The average size of a company was about a dozen or fourteen actors under full-time contract; they could be supplemented by 'hired men'—freelancers—when necessary. Some of Shakespeare's plays are economical in their casting; his early comedy *The Two Gentlemen of Verona* has only thirteen named characters—and a dog. But often he exercised great ingenuity in constructing his plays in such a way that a single actor might play two or more roles within the same play. The early history play *The First Part of the Contention of the Two Famous Houses of York and Lancaster*, otherwise known as *Henry the Sixth, Part Two*, has between seventy and eighty identifiable roles. The backstage area must have been in chaos as actors tried to remember who they were supposed to be, and what they should be wearing to differentiate themselves from the other characters they were playing.

Many actors belonged to the same company for most or all of their careers: for instance the leading man of the Lord Chamberlain's company, Richard Burbage, a founder member in 1594, stayed with it till he died in 1619. This may be why the leading men in Shakespeare's plays—from Romeo through Hamlet, Othello, Macbeth, and Lear to Prospero—tend to age along with him. Actors no doubt had their specialities. Will Kemp, for example, a member from 1594 till around the end of the century, was primarily a comic actor.

Shakespeare often wrote with specific actors in mind. This is clear from the text of *Much Ado About Nothing* printed from his own manuscript in 1600 in which at certain points he had written Kemp's name, along with that of Abraham Cowley, instead of the characters—Dogberry and Verges—they were to impersonate. And he knew his actors' limitations as well as their strengths. Burbage is required to duel and fight in several roles that we know he played, but never to sing except with comic ineptitude as Benedick in *Much Ado About Nothing*. On the other hand Robert Armin, who took over from Kemp, was a musician and is likely to have played such singing roles as Feste, in *Twelfth Night*, the Fool in *King Lear*, and Autolycus in *The Winter's Tale*.

All female roles were played by boys. Cleopatra fears that if she is captured and taken in triumph to Rome she will 'see | Some squeaking Cleopatra boy my greatness | I'th' posture of a whore' (*Antony and Cleopatra*, 5.2.215–17). It was not uncommon for boys to graduate to the stage from choir schools; their ability as singers and their training as performers would have been to their advantage. When exactly a boy stops being a boy and becomes a man may not be entirely easy to determine; in theatrical terms I take it to be when his voice assumes what Arviragus in *Cymbeline* calls 'the mannish crack' (4.2.237) and when his figure and deportment can no longer pass muster as those of a female. At any rate there is no evidence that any male over the age of 20 ever played a woman. Some of Shakespeare's female roles, both comic and tragic, are demanding, but they are limited in number and include few older women. Just to give a few examples, *The Tempest* has only one female role, along with a few goddesses; *Julius Caesar* and *Hamlet* have only two named female roles; *Othello* and *Coriolanus* three; *Romeo and Juliet* four.

On joining a company the boys would have been apprenticed to an adult actor. The companies hung together. Touchingly, Augustine Phillips, one of the Lord Chamberlain's Men, the company for which Shakespeare worked for most of his career, on his death in 1605 bequeathed £5 to be distributed equally among the company's hired men, thirty shillings in gold to his fellows

Shakespeare, Henry Condell, and Christopher Beeston (whose son Augustine may well have been named after Phillips), forty shillings and other bequests to his 'late apprentice Samuel Gilborne', and to 'James Sandes my apprentice' forty shillings and three musical instruments to be handed back to the company at the end of his apprenticeship.

Shakespeare's early career

During his early years in the theatre Shakespeare seems, like many other playwrights of his time, to have worked freelance, sometimes along with other writers. At a time when theatre was expanding rapidly the demand for new plays was high and collaboration was a common practice; around half of the plays surviving from the period were written jointly by two or more authors. The diaries and theatre records of Philip Henslowe, financier of the Lord Admiral's Men, list numerous payments to men—they were always men—who worked alongside one another to create scripts, often under great pressure.

Collaboration could take many different forms. Ben Jonson, in the Prologue to his great, single-authored satirical comedy *Volpone* of 1606, boasts that

> Five weeks fully penned it—
> From his own hand, without a co-adjutor,
> Novice, journeyman, or tutor. (ll. 16–18)

There he usefully defines a range of the roles that a collaborator might perform. A co-adjutor would be an equal collaborator, a novice a kind of apprentice to the master playwright, a journeyman a hack brought in to write under the master's direction, and a tutor a master craftsman guiding a novice. And they could work in a variety of ways: someone would need, perhaps in discussion with his fellows, to choose the story and to work out the overall plotline; after that responsibility for various sections of the dialogue might be allocated to individuals, one perhaps taking responsibility for selected sections of the main story, divided most often into the traditional five-act structure deriving from classical precedent, and one for a subplot; if the authors were working particularly close to one another they could make up the dialogue together as they went along, or revise one another's work as soon as they set it down.

Shakespeare himself seems to have been called in as a kind of playmender to help to revise *The Play of Sir Thomas More* after the Revels Office had demanded substantial revision on political grounds. The play survives in a manuscript of uncertain date which gives us the only example of his handwriting beyond half-a-dozen signatures. He contributed a fine scene (and perhaps another speech). It offers fascinating insight into his methods of composition: his contribution, imperfectly related to what has gone before, includes a passionately eloquent speech by More pleading on behalf of

> wretched strangers [foreigners],
> Their babies at their backs, with their poor luggage,
> Plodding to the ports and coast for transportation.

Clearly written at speed, with few afterthoughts, it is very lightly punctuated (Figure 4).

It is only in recent years that scholars, aided often by computerized linguistic and stylistic analysis, have begun to demonstrate that early in Shakespeare's career, while he was still learning his trade, he worked along with other professional writers. The order in which he wrote the plays, and their dates of composition, are far from clear. But there is good reason to believe, at least, that George Peele (1556–96) was responsible for part of *Titus Andronicus*, especially the first act, perhaps as a direct collaborator or as an original author whose work Shakespeare revised, and that Thomas Nashe had a hand in *Henry the Sixth, Part One*. And in recent years scholars have been

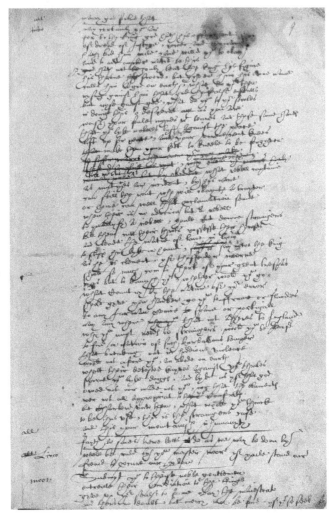

4. A page from the scene from *Sir Thomas More* ascribed to Shakespeare.

supporting the suggestion that the young Shakespeare collaborated in the composition of some plays that have not formed part of the traditional canon of his works, most convincingly *Edward III*, a history play first heard of in 1595, and the domestic tragedy *Arden of Faversham*, printed in 1592.

During this early part of his career Shakespeare was writing—and probably also acting—for more than one company. Plays were written primarily to be acted; many never got into print, and those that did were often published years after they were written. The first of Shakespeare's to reach the bookstalls—though with no mention of him—in 1594, was *Titus Andronicus*, which according to its title page was 'played by the Right Honourable the Earl of Derby, Earl of Pembroke, and Earl of Suffolk their servants'. This may or may not mean that at one time or another he worked, whether as actor or playmaker, for one or more of these companies.

By 1594 Shakespeare had undergone a rigorous and industrious apprenticeship to the craft of playwriting. As well as the sensational but at times profoundly felt tragedy of *Titus Andronicus* he had written the lyrical, romantic comedy of *The Two Gentlemen of Verona*; the far more robust, and more complex, comedy of *The Taming of the Shrew*; the better part of three plays on the reign of Henry the Sixth, culminating in the tragic death of the King; part of the historical tragedy of *Edward III*; and the historical tragedy of *Richard III*.

The narrative poems

His playwriting career suffered serious disruption in 1592 when a terrible outbreak of plague, which was to last for close on two years, caused the authorities of the City of London to close all theatres as a precaution against the spread of infection. Companies could still go on tour, but it was around this time that Shakespeare, apparently feeling the need for an alternative career, embarked on the composition of two long narrative poems, probably conceived as a pair. One, *Venus and Adonis*, is predominantly comic in tone, the other, *The Rape of Lucrece*, tragic. Both were first printed by his fellow Stratfordian Richard Field.

Venus and Adonis is an expansively written mythological poem of 1,194 lines of verse based on a story that Ovid tells in only about 75 lines. The basic story line is simple: Venus, goddess of love, seeks to seduce the beautiful but bashful young mortal Adonis:

> I'll be a park, and thou shalt be my deer;
> Feed where thou wilt, on mountain or in dale;
>> Graze on my lips, and if those hills be dry,
>> Stray lower, where the pleasant fountains lie.

But Adonis prefers boar hunting. He takes to the chase as a respite from Venus' remorseless attentions; she nervously awaits his return from the hunt, hears the yelping of his hounds, sees a bloodstained boar, comes upon Adonis' defeated dogs, and at last finds his bloodstained body with a fatal wound in his flank. Shakespeare tells the slight story in six-line stanzas rhymed like the final section of a sonnet. The tone is generally light, often witty, rising to largely monosyllabic eloquence in the final grief-laden account of Venus' mourning:

> She looks upon his lips, and they are pale.
> She takes him by the hand, and that is cold.
> She whispers in his ears a heavy tale,
> As if they heard the woeful words she told.
>> She lifts the coffer-lids that close his eyes,
>> Where lo, two lamps burnt out in darkness lies . . . (ll. 1123–8)

Poems of this kind were just becoming popular with Elizabethan readers. Christopher Marlowe, who died in the year Shakespeare's poem was published, had written his beautiful and erotic masterpiece *Hero and Leander* not long before; it was not printed until 1598, but poems commonly circulated in manuscript and Shakespeare may well have read it before publication. He certainly knew it soon afterwards because he quotes its most famous line in *As You Like It*, around 1599 or 1600. Referring to Marlowe as a 'dead shepherd'—because of his associations with pastoral poetry—he makes Phoebe say:

Dead shepherd, now I find thy saw of might [i.e. your saying to be powerful]— 'Whoever loved that loved not at first sight?' (3.5.82–3)

Plague remorselessly continued and in the following year, 1594, Shakespeare's second narrative poem, *The Rape of Lucrece*, also based on a poem by Ovid, appeared. Deadly serious and powerfully erotic in tone, this seems conceived as a tragic counterpart to the comedy of its precursor. Historical rather than mythological, it opens dramatically with a terse description of Tarquin's departure from the Roman camp determined to seek out and violate the chaste Lucrece:

> From the besieged Ardea all in post,
> Borne by the trustless wings of false desire,
> Lust-breathèd Tarquin leaves the Roman host
> And to Collatium bears the lightless fire
> Which, in pale embers hid, lurks to aspire
> > And girdle with embracing flames the waist
> > Of Collatine's fair love, Lucrece the chaste.

The long opening sequence leading up to the rape gives an intensely dramatic account of Tarquin's tormented state of mind as he approaches Lucrece's chamber. Many years later Shakespeare was to refer to 'Tarquin's ravishing strides' in *Macbeth* (2.1.55), another profound study in evil. The emotional temperature of the poem goes down in its later stages, when Lucrece addresses night, time, and opportunity in a series of laments and curses Tarquin before deciding to kill herself for shame and to tell her husband what has happened.

Venus and Adonis and *The Rape of Lucrece*, comparatively little read today, were phenomenally successful in their time and were reprinted far more frequently than any of Shakespeare's plays. Around 1600 a Cambridge scholar, Gabriel Harvey, wrote that 'the younger sort take much pleasure in Shakespeare's *Venus and Adonis*, but his *Lucrece*, and his tragedy of *Hamlet Prince of Denmark*, have it in them to please the wiser sort'. *Venus and Adonis*, along with Marlowe's *Hero and Leander*, acquired a reputation as soft porn; a character in a play performed by Cambridge students early in the 17th century boasts of how he woos his mistress with speeches larded with quotations from *Romeo and Juliet* and *Venus and Adonis*, and declares that he will 'worship sweet master Shakespeare, and to honour him will lay his *Venus and Adonis* under my pillow'. Similarly a recently married husband in a play by Thomas Middleton, *A Mad World My Masters* (1608), boasts that he has taken away from his wife 'all her wanton pamphlets, as *Hero and Leander*, *Venus and Adonis*', clearly regarding them as potential incitements to lechery.

Though we assume that Shakespeare was writing these poems in an attempt to keep himself—and his family—afloat financially, we don't know how much money he made out of them; copyright did not exist, and publishers were more concerned to make profits for themselves than for their authors. A clue may lie in the fact that both poems bear a dedication (Figure 5) printed over Shakespeare's name to Henry Wriothesley, the third Earl of Southampton, an androgynous and highly intelligent beauty some ten years younger than Shakespeare. The first dedication is relatively formal in tone, the second much warmer, suggesting that a real friendship may have developed. In any case it was customary for dedicatees to reward their authors with sums of money. This was usually no more than a couple of guineas or so, but the Earl was exceptionally generous—and extravagant. He has often been thought to be the so-called fair young boy or man to whom some of Shakespeare's sonnets are addressed (although there may well have been more than one such person).

TO THE RIGHT

HONOVRABLE, HENRY
VVriotheſley, Earle of Southhampton,
and Baron of Titchfield.

HE loue I dedicate to your
Lordſhip is without end:wher-
of this Pamphlet without beginning is but a ſuperfluous
Moity. The warrant I haue of
your Honourable diſpoſition,
not the worth of my vntutord
Lines makes it aſſured of acceptance. VVhat I haue
done is yours, what I haue to doe is yours, being
part in all I haue, deuoted yours. VVere my worth
greater, my duety would ſhew greater, meane time,
as it is,it is bound to your Lordſhip; To whom I wiſh
long life ſtill lengthned with all happineſſe.

Your Lordſhips in all duety.

William Shakeſpeare.

A 2

5. The dedication to *Lucrece* (1594).

The Lord Chamberlain's, later the King's Men

In June 1594, the plague having abated, London's theatres reopened and a new acting company was formed under the patronage of Queen Elizabeth's Lord Chamberlain, Henry Carey, First Baron Hunsdon. Shakespeare appears to have been a member from the start: on 15 March of the following year he is named as joint payee, along with the actors William Kemp and Richard Burbage, for two performances given before the Queen at Greenwich during the previous Christmas season. It was a milestone in his career. No longer a freelance at the beck and call of whoever would employ him, he was his own man, a full-time member, as actor, writer, and shareholder, of a prestigious and successful company. For at least the next ten years all his plays are of single authorship, and for the rest of his career he wrote for no other company. And, as we have seen, his finances prospered to such an extent that within three years he was able to set up his family in New Place, Stratford-upon-Avon.

His reputation grew rapidly. In 1598 his name first appeared on the title pages of any of his plays, and in a book called *Palladis Tamia, or Wit's Treasury* by Francis Meres (a chronicler rather than a critic of any distinction), he is described as 'the most excellent' for comedy and tragedy 'among the English . . . for the stage'. And, most conveniently, Meres names as comedies *The Two Gentlemen of Verona*, *The Comedy of Errors*, *Love's Labour's Lost*, *Love's Labour's Won*, *A Midsummer Night's Dream*, and *The Merchant of Venice*; and as tragedies, *Richard II*, *Richard III*, *Henry IV*, *King John*, *Titus Andronicus*, and *Romeo and Juliet*. The list is invaluable because it mentions some of these plays for the first time, helping us to know by what date they were written. It also presents a puzzle: no play called *Love's Labour's Won* survives. The title also occurs in a bookseller's list of around 1603, so it may be a lost play by Shakespeare.

The exact terms of Shakespeare's responsibilities for the Lord Chamberlain's Men, and of his rewards for his work for the company, are not known. He certainly acted for them. His name occurs as an actor in the character lists of two plays by Ben Jonson, *Every Man in his Humour* (acted in 1598) and *Sejanus* (1603), and heads the list of 'the names of the principal actors in all these plays' in his own First Folio of 1623. But we don't know for certain any of the parts that he played, and he seems to have had no great reputation as an actor.

He certainly worked hard for the company as a writer, keeping up an average of around two plays a year, and supplying a well-varied mixture of plays of various kinds. The company prospered, often playing at court before the Queen (who never attended the public theatres). And Shakespeare prospered along with it, as is clear from the substantial investments he made in his home town. In 1599, when the Globe playhouse went up, he is named among the men responsible for building and running it, and was a substantial shareholder.

When King James I succeeded Queen Elizabeth in 1603 the Lord Chamberlain's Men became the King's Men; Shakespeare is named among the nine members of the company in the royal warrants for the letters patent, in the letters themselves, and in a document granting each member of the company four-and-a-half yards of scarlet cloth to be worn in the Coronation procession. By this time he had added to his early plays and to those named by Meres the culminating play of his second history cycle, *Henry V*, the successful Roman tragedy *Julius Caesar*, acted at the Globe in 1599, the domestic comedy *The Merry Wives of Windsor*, which seems to have been written for a specific occasion, perhaps for performance at Windsor Castle as well as in public playhouses, the two greatest of his romantic comedies, *As You Like It* and *Twelfth Night*, the bitter, tragicomic *Troilus and Cressida*, and the immensely successful (and long) tragedy of *Hamlet*. It is during this period that he makes most use of prose in his plays.

From around the time of King James's accession Shakespeare's plays take on a darker tone. This is probably not a matter of cause and effect, more probably a reflection of his mental, emotional, and spiritual development. *Measure for Measure* and *All's Well That Ends Well*, though comic in form, treat of serious moral and ethical problems. The tragedies of *Othello*, *Macbeth*, and *King Lear* are more sombre in tone and have less of a redemptive quality than *Hamlet*. And, for some reason unknown to us, round about 1606 Shakespeare started once more to work in collaboration with other playwrights, all younger than he.

The tragedy of *Timon of Athens*, not quite complete in the text that has come down to us, is partly the work of Thomas Middleton (1580–1627), who, along with Ben Jonson, was gradually becoming the greatest dramatist of the generation after Shakespeare. And around 1607 Shakespeare wrote parts of *Pericles* along with George Wilkins (*c.*1576–1618), an unsavoury keeper of inns that doubled as brothels, sole author of only one other play, *The Miseries of Enforced Marriage*, which had been acted by the King's Men at around the same time. But Shakespeare continued to write single-authored plays, to develop his artistry in new ways that both demonstrate his versatility and enable him to continue serving the needs of his company of players. Two more Roman tragedies, the ravishingly poetic *Antony and Cleopatra* and the austere *Coriolanus*, are stylistically worlds apart from one another. And the new vein of romance drama that he had begun to tap in *Pericles* flowered in three more single-authored masterpieces of the kind, *The Winter's Tale*, *Cymbeline*, and *The Tempest*. Late in his career too he took on a new collaborator, John Fletcher (1579–1625), fifteen years his junior, who had already proved his worth in a number of single-authored plays and in others written along with Francis Beaumont (1584–1616); together Shakespeare and Fletcher wrote the historical drama about the reign of Henry VIII, *All is True*, *The Two Noble Kinsmen*, and the lost *Cardenio*.

6. The Blackfriars Playhouse, Staunton, Virginia.

The dramaturgy of some of Shakespeare's late plays was influenced by the fact that from 1609 the King's Men were able to make use of an indoor theatre, the Blackfriars. Considerably smaller than the Globe, illuminated by candlelight, appealing because of its high admission prices to a more exclusive clientele, famous for the quality of its musicians, this playhouse offered more facilities for special effects than the Globe, as can be seen in for example Shakespeare's use of flying devices in *Cymbeline* and *The Tempest*. It is possible, however, to exaggerate the effect of the new building on his work; plays still had to be performed in the summer, at least, in the Globe, and to be taken on tour. Attempts to reproduce features of the Blackfriars can be seen in the Sam Wanamaker Playhouse which is part of London's Bankside Globe complex, and in the Blackfriars Playhouse in Staunton, Virginia (Figure 6).

Chapter 3
Shakespeare in London

We know more about Shakespeare's professional than about his private life during the years in which his career centred on the capital. Prosperous though he became, he seems to have lived modestly, ploughing the bulk of his earnings back into investments in his home town. In 1597 he is listed as having moved out of lodgings in the parish of St Helen's Bishopsgate, fairly close to the northerly theatre district, without having paid his taxes late in the previous year. There is a sighting of him in the same parish the following year. His goods were valued at the modest sum of £5. A year or so later he seems to have moved to Southwark to be closer to the Globe.

Then early in the 17th century, probably in 1602, he moved north of the river again. We know this because of a court case which gives us the most detailed record of his personal life in the capital. In 1612, described as 'William Shakespeare of Stratford-upon-Avon', he was called on to give evidence relating to events dating back to 1604. He had been lodging then in Silver Street, close to the most northerly part of London Wall, in the household of Christopher Mountjoy, a Huguenot refugee whose wife and daughter made ladies' wigs and headdresses. Shakespeare, who had lodged in the house for around two years, had good-naturedly assisted in negotiations relating to the daughter's marriage to

Mountjoy's apprentice, Stephen Belott; a witness said that the lovers 'were made sure by Master Shakespeare by giving their consent, and agreed to marry, and did marry', which sounds as if he had officiated at the informal but legally binding ceremony known as handfasting. In *As You Like It* (4.1.116–31) Celia performs this service for Orlando and Rosalind, disguised as Ganymede.

The law case arose because some years later Belott accused his father-in-law of breaking promises to pay his daughter a marriage portion of £60 and to leave her £200 in his will. Shakespeare said in court that they 'had had among themselves many conferences [conversations] about their marriage which afterwards was consummated and solemnised', but that he knew nothing about 'what implements and household stuff' Mountjoy gave Belott on his marriage. The case shows Shakespeare in a good light and gives us our only direct record of words that he actually spoke. Sadly they are not particularly characterful.

Gossip about his private life in London was recorded by a young law student at the Middle Temple, John Manningham, who kept a diary. On 13 March 1602, he recorded a scurrilous anecdote about Shakespeare and Burbage:

> Upon a time, when Burbage played Richard III, there was a citizen
> [he means a woman, a citizen's wife] grew so far in liking with
> him that before she went from the play she appointed him to come
> that night unto her by the name of Richard III. Shakespeare,
> overhearing their conclusion, went before, was entertained, and at
> his game ere Burbage came. Then, message being brought that
> Richard the Third was at the door, Shakespeare caused return to be
> made that William the Conqueror came before Richard the Third.

It is a good story, and may even be true.

Shakespeare's sonnets

Shakespeare's plays, and his narrative poems, too, were public works, written in part, at least, to make money, manifestations of his professional persona. But frequently, it would seem, he composed poems for his own pleasure, or to work out emotional situations in which he was involved without expecting to publish them, and with no expectation of profit, always in the form of the sonnet with which as a young lover he had expressed relief at the resolution of his tiff with Anne Hathaway. The first we hear of them is in the book of 1598 by Francis Meres, *Palladis Tamia*, which also praises his plays. Somehow Meres knew that Shakespeare had written what he calls 'sugared sonnets among his private friends'. He may mean by this that they circulated privately, or even that they were addressed to his intimates. Two sonnets got into print in a slim, catchpenny volume called *The Passionate Pilgrim* which appeared over Shakespeare's name in 1599. It also included three extracts from *Love's Labour's Lost* and fifteen other poems, amorous and mildly erotic, some definitely not by Shakespeare, others whose authors have not been identified. The publisher, William Jaggard, was capitalizing on Shakespeare's reputation.

Ten years later, in 1609, another publisher, Thomas Thorpe, somehow got hold of a collection of 154 sonnets by Shakespeare, along with a narrative poem called 'A Lover's Complaint', and published them as 'Shakespeare's Sonnets, never before Imprinted'. He composed an enigmatic dedication to the volume which reads 'To the only begetter of these ensuing sonnets Mr W. H. all happiness and that eternity promised by our ever-living poet wisheth the well-wishing adventurer in setting forth' and appeared over his own initials—T.T.

The sonnets include some of the most beautiful and popular love poems in English, some of which might equally be addressed to, or be inspired by, a male or a female, young or not so young. They tell of the power of love and of friendship to convey happiness, to transcend time, to confer a kind of immortality on the loved one. 'Shall I compare thee to a summer's day? | Thou art more lovely and more temperate', says the poet in No. 18. In No. 29,

> Haply I think on thee, and then my state,
> Like to the lark at break of day arising
> From sullen earth, sings hymns at heaven's gate.
>> For thy sweet love remembered such wealth brings
>> That then I scorn to change my state with kings.'

And No. 116, beginning 'Let me not to the marriage of true minds | Admit impediments', is a great hymn to love:

> It is the star to every wand'ring barque,
> Whose worth's unknown although his height be taken.

But other poems in the collection are very different in tone. Some speak of rivalry: 'Two loves I have, of comfort and despair, | Which like two spirits do suggest me still. | The better angel is a man right fair, | The worser spirit a woman coloured ill' (144). Some tell of disillusionment and self-deception in love: 'When my love swears that she is made of truth | I do believe her though I know she lies' (138); 'For I have sworn thee fair, and thought thee bright, | Who art as black as hell, as dark as night' (147). In some the poet abases himself before the beloved: 'Canst thou, O cruel, say I love thee not | When I against myself with thee partake?' (149). In others he writes with self-disgust of his enthralment to someone he feels is unworthy of him: 'My love is as a fever, longing still | For that which longer nurseth the disease' (147). No. 129 expresses shame at sexual enthralment: 'Th'expense of spirit in a waste of shame | Is lust in action.' And whereas in 146 the poet writes that the soul can be enriched by bodily decay—'Then, soul, live thou upon thy servant's loss, | Buy terms divine in selling hours of dross'—in 151 he writes with exultant obscenity that

> thou betraying me, I do betray
> My nobler part to my gross body's treason.
> My soul doth tell my body that he may
> Triumph in love; flesh stays no further reason,
> But rising at thy name doth point out thee
> As his triumphant prize.

In the poem's closing lines the poet leaves no doubt about what part of his body he means by 'flesh':

> Proud of this prize,
> He is contented thy poor drudge to be,
> To stand in thy affairs, fall by thy side.
> No want of conscience hold it that I call
> Her 'love' for whose dear love I rise and fall.

It looks as if Shakespeare himself put the poems into the order in which they are printed.

There is nothing to suggest that he had anything to do with the publication of the volume. Its title is in the third person—'*Shakespeare's Sonnets*', not e.g. '*Sonnets*, by William Shakespeare'—and the dedication was written by the publisher, not by the author. Over the centuries its contents have been seriously misunderstood and misrepresented.

There had been a fashion during the 1590s for the writing and publication of unified sequences of sonnets in praise of an individual addressee. This gave rise to false assumptions about Shakespeare's sonnets. Among the first 126 are some that relate to one or more young men, addressed variously as 'beauteous and lovely youth' (54), 'sweet boy' (108), 'my lovely boy' (126); all the sonnets that clearly relate to one or more women are printed among the remaining 28. Assumptions that Shakespeare was writing a unified sequence have led to the supposition that the first group tells of a real or imagined love for one young man, and that the second tells of his love for a 'dark lady'. In fact the poems were written, sometimes singly, sometimes in interrelated batches, over a long period of time. It looks as if Shakespeare was writing in these poems about a number of different friends and lovers.

Unlike the narrative poems the volume was a flop. It was not reprinted until 1640, and then in a garbled fashion. The Sonnets were little known or admired until the Romantic period, and even then, especially in Victorian times, many readers regarded them with distaste for their homoerotic implications, explored by Oscar Wilde in his story 'The Portrait of Mr W.H.' (1889).

Shakespeare's last years

Is it just coincidence that Shakespeare's writing career seems to have come to an end around the time that the Globe burnt down, in June 1613, or did the disaster affect him so deeply that he had not the heart to go on writing plays? Or was he simply played out? His last single-authored play, *The Tempest*, is somewhat valedictory in tone, and though it is sentimental to see Prospero as a self-portrait, the character—father, artist, surrogate playwright, conjuror up of visions—has points in common with its author.

The Globe was rapidly rebuilt, this time with a tiled rather a thatched roof, and the King's Men went on performing Shakespeare's and other dramatists' plays there. Burbage died suddenly in 1619, deeply mourned; the Earl of Pembroke, who with his brother the Earl of Montgomery was to be a dedicatee of the First Folio, was so deeply affected that he could not bring himself to join in the festivities at a great banquet held a couple of months later, writing of them that 'I, being tender-hearted, could not endure to see so soon after the loss of my old acquaintance Burbage'. The evening was to have ended with a performance of *Pericles* in which very likely Burbage had been accustomed to play the title role.

The second Globe survived as a working playhouse until the closing of the theatres of 1642. When playing was resumed in 1660, on the accession of King Charles II, it was in indoor theatres with perspective scenery and with women playing female roles. The texts of the plays began to be adapted to suit the new playing conditions, and a new chapter in the story of Shakespeare's reputation began.

The First Folio

In 1623 the volume known today as the First Folio brought together thirty-six of Shakespeare's plays along with commendatory poems by friends and former colleagues, most notably Ben Jonson's fine tribute 'To the memory of my beloved the author, Master William Shakespeare, and what he hath left us', which includes the words 'He was not of an [one] age, but for all time.' It includes plays, such as *Henry VIII*, known when it was first performed as *All is True*, in which Shakespeare collaborated with another playwright—in this case presumably because the play completes a sequence of English histories—but omits others, such as *Pericles* and *Edward III*, in which we now believe that Shakespeare had a hand.

The Folio opens with an 'epistle dedicatory' to Burbage's admirer William Earl of Pembroke, eminent patron of the arts who as Lord Chamberlain had special responsibility for court entertainments, and to his brother Philip Earl of Montgomery, signed by John Heminges and Henry Condell. It may be relevant that, as I have said, in his will of 1616 Shakespeare had left money to buy mourning rings to these former colleagues of long standing along with Richard Burbage, who died in 1619. It seems possible that before he died he had helped to plan the volume with these men, or at least that he had discussed it with them. The only English playwright whose work had previously been gathered together like this was Jonson himself, in 1616.

The Folio is immensely important because half of the plays it includes are printed there for the first time. Without it we should almost certainly be without some of Shakespeare's greatest plays, including *Twelfth Night*, *As You Like It*, *Macbeth*, *Antony and Cleopatra*, and *The Winter's Tale*. It does not include any of Shakespeare's poems, perhaps for copyright reasons.

The Folio has had a profound effect on the way Shakespeare's plays have been received since its publication, not entirely to their benefit. Tidy-mindedly, it divides them into three categories: histories (in fact only plays about English history), comedies, and tragedies. The latter two categories refer to dramatic form, but the first, 'histories', relates to subject matter. Some of Shakespeare's plays about English history, such as *Richard II* and *Richard III*, are tragic in form and subject matter; others, especially *Henry V*, which ends happily both with a victory for the English army and with the King's betrothal to the Princess of France, are closer to comedies. The Folio's imposition of categories is regrettable because it gives the impression that Shakespeare was more wedded to neo-classical theories of dramatic form than his practice suggests.

Eighteen of the Folio plays had previously appeared in print, mostly in the form of small paperback books known as quartos. Although the Folio versions of some of these are simple reprints of the original edition with only small changes, others are printed either from texts that had been heavily altered by comparison with a different, theatrically based manuscript, or at least partially from independent manuscripts. It is only in recent years that scholars have recognized that, for example, the variations between the texts of *Othello*, *Hamlet*, *King Lear*, and *Troilus and Cressida* show that Shakespeare, no doubt working along with his actors, changed his mind about some of his plays when they were put into production, sometimes cutting speeches or even whole scenes, sometimes adding them, sometimes making tiny or more substantial changes in the dialogue, at other times moving a speech from one character to another. He was a practical man of the theatre, aware of the capabilities and limitations of his actors and of the demands of his audiences.

The other main way in which the Folio's presentation of the plays has affected their reception is the attempt, not fully carried through, to impose on them act and scene divisions. This again seeks to imitate the practice of classical dramatists such as those whose plays Shakespeare would have studied at school. The texts of plays that had been printed separately before the Folio show that although Shakespeare was aware of the five-act structure of classical drama—as *Henry V*, with its series of Choruses before each act, shows—he was far more inclined to think in terms of scenes and of overall structure than of acts. The Folio's neo-classicizing of the text savours strongly of Ben Jonson, who may have exerted a quasi-editorial function on the compilers of the Folio. Although we have become accustomed to using traditional act and scene divisions as a convenient reference system, most modern editors of the plays increasingly try to minimize their impact on readers, even abandoning them altogether in some instances.

Obviously, Shakespeare himself had nothing to do with the printing of the First Folio—though it is not impossible that he envisaged and even, in his last days, helped to plan its publication. Most of the texts it presents lie at several removes from his manuscripts. The way the plays are presented in its pages—their spelling, their punctuation, their use of capital letters, their layout on the page—was the responsibility mainly of the workmen in the printing house and, for some plays, of scribes who were paid to make copies for use in the theatre or for publication. The common idea that modern actors can be helped by paying attention to such details in early editions is mistaken. Even the stage directions of some of the early texts do not come directly from Shakespeare. It is desirable for all except specialist readers to read the plays in responsibly prepared modern editions in order to come close to experiencing them as authentically as possible.

Where do the plays come from?

Rather naughtily, though entirely characteristically, George Bernard Shaw praised Shakespeare's 'gift of telling a story (provided that someone else told it to him first)'. It is not an entirely unfair remark. Books were all-important to Shakespeare as a stimulus to his imagination and as a source for the stories of his plays. This may be partly because, in an age of only partial literacy, the drama was seen as an instrument of education. We should not patronize the audiences of the time. They made popular some of the most intellectually and emotionally demanding plays ever written; but some theatregoers may have been unable to read, and plays would have provided a way of introducing them to the myths and legends of ancient times, the narratives of Greek and Roman history, and the past of their own country.

But books were important to Shakespeare also because he could use familiar stories to create theatrically effective situations, to entertain, amuse, and move his audiences, to explore the intricacies of human behaviour, and to provide intellectual stimulus. It is to these ends that he borrows the narrative material of almost all his plays from books, whether fictional, legendary, mythical, historical, or theatrical. He had a preference for the past and for the geographically remote, which freed his imagination from the claims of actuality, allowing it to operate in worlds of myth and symbol. This helps to explain his enduring popularity: his plays are not tied down to topics that would have been of interest only to audiences of his own day.

To say that Shakespeare told stories that had already been told is not however to say that he borrowed the plots of his plays. The layout and structuring of their stories, the ways in which they are plotted in dramatic form, the perspectives from which their stories are told, the disposition of the scenes, the juxtaposition of plot with subplot, the varying of the action with the inclusion of songs and other set pieces, the presentation of their narratives sometimes with choric figures as presenters, the inclusion of prologues, epilogues, and plays within plays—all these are of Shakespeare's own invention, ways in which he transmutes his inherited raw material into the stuff of original drama.

How Shakespeare worked

Shakespeare was constantly experimenting with dramatic form, and with the conventions of theatre. This is partly for practical reasons: his company needed a stream of new plays, and it was important that their house dramatist should not repeat himself. But it is also because Shakespeare had a developing mind, an imagination that would not be satisfied with formulaic repetition. He was writing for himself as well as for his audiences, digging deeper and deeper into his innermost imaginative resources, willing sometimes to challenge both his actors and his audiences, to risk unpopularity rather than to go on producing a series of potboilers.

This means that his plays are often difficult to categorize. Those that are based on English and classical history draw variously on the conventions and techniques of both comedy and tragedy. Plays that are primarily tragic in tone may be shot through with comedy, as *Hamlet* most conspicuously is. Plays in comic form, especially those written later in Shakespeare's career, often contain deeply serious elements.

Partly for this reason it is difficult to generalize about Shakespeare's artistry. Each play represents a step forward in his artistic, even his spiritual development, and in each play he adopted different technical means to achieve his artistic ends. In Chapters 4–8 I offer a brief introduction to each play, sketching its origins, stories, and themes. I also touch on aspects of Shakespeare's techniques and artistry and of the ways in which, over his quarter-century long career, he developed his long sequence of plays from history, from literature of the past and of his own time, and from his powers of invention. Rather than discussing them in the order in which they were written (not always easy to ascertain) I have grouped related plays together without necessarily following the traditional categories. A chronological table at the back of the book lists the works in approximate order of composition.

Chapter 4
Plays of the 1590s

History plays

During the first eight or ten years of Shakespeare's career he wrote a series of more or less closely interrelated plays based on English history drawing heavily, as I have said, on Holinshed's *Chronicles* and other accounts. These plays show a deeply serious concern with political problems, with the responsibilities of a king, his relationship with the people, the need for national unity, the relationship between national welfare and self-interest, and the suffering caused by strife both between nations and between opposing factions within a nation, often mirrored in the image of a family, whether royal or not.

But Shakespeare was primarily an artist and an entertainer rather than an instructor. In the earlier plays especially, while his education was still fresh in his mind, he draws extensively on current literary and poetic conventions such as pastoral and epic poetry, and on the techniques and forms of rhetoric and oratory that he had learned at school, while also using and helping to develop the techniques of historical drama. In the later-written plays his powers of invention have fuller play and his treatment of history becomes correspondingly more inventive.

Henry VI, Parts One to Three, and Richard III

Shakespeare probably did not know as he started to write his history plays that they would eventually include two more or less closely interrelated groups of four plays each, sometimes known as tetralogies; nevertheless the first four especially gain greatly in dramatic effectiveness when played (with a bit of textual adjustment) as a sequence.

They offer many powerful acting roles both within individual plays and spanning more than one, especially that of the seductive and powerful Margaret of Anjou, who is wooed on behalf of King Henry VI in the first play and remains as an aged figure of retributive justice to curse his murderer, Richard III, in the last. Over the four plays this can add up to one of Shakespeare's strongest female roles.

The three plays based on the life of King Henry VI and culminating in the King's murder are best described as chronicle histories. In them historical events take prominence over dramatic form. But the fourth play, *Richard III*, centring on the rise and fall of the King, casts history into tragic form, drawing the threads together in its final scene when the ghosts of all Richard's victims rise from the dead to curse him and to bless his successor, Henry VII.

The Henry VI plays were written out of chronological sequence. The last composed—a great success in its own time—was *Henry VI, Part One*, in which Shakespeare appears to have collaborated with Thomas Nashe. The authors pack in a mass of material, some historical, some invented. The play opens impressively with the funeral of Henry V, celebrated for conquering France and unifying England; but his nobles are already at loggerheads even over his coffin, and news arrives of serious losses in France. The rivalry between Humphrey, Duke of Gloucester, Protector of the infant Henry VI, and Henry Beaufort,

Bishop of Winchester, plays an important part both in this play and in the one that continues the action, entitled on its first printing *The First Part of the Contention of the Two Famous Houses of York and Lancaster,* as does that between Richard, Duke of York, and the houses of Somerset and Suffolk. Their supporters symbolize their respective loyalties in the emblematic and formalized scene set in the Temple Garden (2.4)—still to be seen in London—which Shakespeare invented, by plucking white (for York) and red roses. This scene establishes the opposition between the houses of York and Lancaster which will not be resolved until the closing lines of *Richard III.* Their enmity weakens the country's strength, but she has a great hero in Lord Talbot, whose nobility as a warrior is pitted against the treachery of the French, led by King Charles and the whorish witch Joan la Pucelle—the maid of France, later portrayed in very different colours by George Bernard Shaw in *St Joan.* History is freely manipulated for dramatic effect. Joan was burnt in 1431, though the authors have her take part in a battle of 1451 in which Talbot's death is brought forward by two years.

Henry VI himself spends most of his time on stage in well-meaning but pathetically inadequate attempts to make peace among his brawling nobles. In the closing scenes he timorously agrees to marry Margaret, whom he has not so far seen, in the hope that this will help to bring England and France together. The play ends with an uneasy peace between the two countries.

The First Part of the Contention, later known as *Henry VI, Part Two,* dramatizes the touchingly weak king's powerlessness against the machinations of his nobles, especially the ambitious Richard, Duke of York. Henry's saintly ineffectuality is seen to be the cause of both personal and national disaster. His acceptance of the terms negotiated by Suffolk for his marriage, by which England loses territory to France, infuriates his Protector, Humphrey, Duke of Gloucester, and causes a renewal of the 'ancient bickerings' (1.1.142) between him and Cardinal Beaufort, Bishop of

Winchester; while Henry's elevation of Suffolk (who appears to be his wife's lover) to a dukedom and his demotion of York from his post of Regent of France feed York's ambition to usurp him:

> I'll make him yield the crown,
> Whose bookish rule hath pulled fair England down. (1.1.258–9)

Women play an important part in this play; the rivalry between Queen Margaret and the Duchess of Gloucester produces comic bickerings as well as politically serious consequences. And the common people, who figure hardly at all in *Part One*, are prominent. Richard engineers the Kentish rebellion, led by Jack Cade, which provides some of the play's liveliest episodes, written mostly in vigorous and characterful prose. 'The first thing we do let's kill all the lawyers', says a butcher (4.2.78). Finally Richard, addressed already as a 'foul indigested lump, | As crookèd in thy manners as thy shape!' (5.1.155–6), seems poised to ascend the throne. This play, in which historical events are dramatized with comparative fidelity to historical fact within a coherent structure, offers a wider variety of theatrical entertainment than its fellows.

Third comes the play published originally under the cumbersome title of *The True Tragedy of Richard Duke of York, and the Death of Good King Henry the Sixth, with the Whole Contention between the two Houses Lancaster and York*, later known as *Henry VI, Part Three*. This takes up the story where *The Contention* ends, with the aspirations of Richard, Duke of York, to the English throne. Again history is manipulated for dramatic effect. The final scenes of the earlier play have introduced York's sons, Edward and Richard, who, along with their brothers Edmund, Earl of Rutland, and George (later Duke of Clarence), figure more prominently in *The True Tragedy*. In the opening scenes York seems to be on the way to fulfilling his ambition, but Margaret, far more warrior-like than her husband, leads an army against York and when he is captured taunts him in a superbly rhetorical episode with news of the murder of his youngest son, stabs him to death, and commands that his head be 'set on York's gates'. It makes for great theatre.

Before long, York's sons are in the ascendant. The balance of power shifts frequently and the brothers' alliance crumbles, but finally Margaret is defeated and captured, and Richard's surviving sons avenge their father's death by killing her son Edward before her eyes. Richard of Gloucester starts to clear his way to the throne by murdering 'good King Henry' in the Tower, and the play ends with the new King Edward exulting in his 'country's peace and brothers' loves' while Richard makes clear to the audience that Edward's self-confidence is ill-founded.

Though this play is strife-ridden with war, power politics, and personal ambition, a concern with humane values emerges in the touching and subtle continuing portrayal of the quietist Henry VI, a saintly fool who meditates on the superiority of humble contentment to regal misery in an emblematic scene that epitomizes the tragedy of civil strife. Shakespeare gives him a long, highly formalized, and lyrically beautiful meditation drawing on the techniques of pastoral verse in which he contrasts the life of a king with that of a shepherd:

> Gives not the hawthorn bush a sweeter shade
> To shepherds looking on their seely [harmless] sheep
> Than doth a rich embroidered canopy
> To kings that fear their subjects' treachery?
> O yes, it doth—a thousandfold it doth.
> And to conclude, the shepherd's homely curds,
> His cold thin drink out of his leather bottle,
> His wonted sleep under a fresh tree's shade,
> All which secure and sweetly he enjoys,
> Is far beyond a prince's delicates,
> His viands sparkling in a golden cup,
> His body couchèd in a curious bed,
> When care, mistrust, and treason waits on him.

(2.5.42–54)

The final play of this first sequence, *Richard III*, based on Sir Thomas More's *History of King Richard the Third* as incorporated in the chronicles of Holinshed and Edward Hall, is strongly influenced also by the tragedies of the Roman dramatist Seneca (*c*.4 BC–AD 65), with their ghosts, rhetorical style, and their indirect, highly formal presentation of violence—apart from the stabbing of Clarence in 1.4 there is no on-stage violence in *Richard III* until its final scenes. Here Shakespeare shapes history more completely to an overall design than in the earlier history plays. Richard—one of his greatest gifts to the acting profession—is a more centrally dominating figure than any that have gone before, historical events are more freely handled, and the play's language is even more highly patterned and rhetorically unified.

Shakespeare invents the highly stylized episode of Richard's wooing of Lady Anne over her father-in-law's coffin (1.2) and causes Queen Margaret, who historically had gone back to France and died, to remain alive in England as a choric figure of grief and retribution. The episodes in which the Duchess of York, Queen Elizabeth, and Queen Margaret bemoan their losses, along with the climactic procession of ghosts before the final confrontation of Richard with the idealized figure of Richmond, the future Henry VII, help to make this play the culmination of a tetralogy as well as a masterpiece in its own right. The dominance of Richard is one reason why this play may be thought of as a historical tragedy rather than a chronicle history. It has come to be regarded as a great showpiece, a vehicle for virtuosity; an actor coming to the role can scarcely fail to remember William Hazlitt's description of Edmund Kean (1787–1833) in the death scene: 'He fought like one drunk with wounds: and the attitude in which he stands with his hands stretched out, after his sword is taken from him, had a preternatural and terrific grandeur, as if his will could not be disarmed, and the very phantoms of his despair had a withering power.' In the final speech Richmond, now King Henry VII, heir to the house of Lancaster and grandfather of the reigning Queen Elizabeth I at the time the play was written, proclaims that 'peace lives again', and prays 'That she may long live here, God say "Amen"', providing a patriotic climax to the entire tetralogy that must have been immensely stirring to the play's original audiences.

Titus Andronicus and Romeo and Juliet

Tragedies were conventionally based on history. Shakespeare's first tragedy not to be based on English history, *Titus Andronicus*, now believed to have been written in part by George Peele, is set vaguely in the 4th century BC, but tells a fictitious story that its authors may have invented. Dating from Shakespeare's freelance period, it was printed in 1594 (except for the powerful and emblematic Act 3 Scene 2, a later addition first found in the 1623 Folio). Ovid, whose *Metamorphoses* appears on stage (4.1), influenced its spirit, style, and some incidents of the plot. A great success in its own time, it came to be regarded as a blot on Shakespeare's reputation, a barbaric piece of brutal sensationalism pandering to the lowest tastes of contemporary playgoers.

It tells a story of double revenge. Tamora, Queen of the Goths, seeks revenge on her captor, Titus, for the ritual slaughter of her son Alarbus; she achieves it when her other sons, Chiron and Demetrius, rape and horrifically mutilate Titus' daughter Lavinia. Later, Titus himself seeks revenge on Tamora and her husband Saturninus after her black lover, Aaron, has falsely led him to believe that he can save his sons' lives by allowing his own hand to be chopped off. Though Titus is driven to madness, he, along with his brother Marcus and his last surviving son, Lucius, achieves a spectacular sequence of vengeance in which he slits Tamora's sons' throats, serves their flesh baked in a pie to their mother, kills Lavinia so as to save her from her shame, and stabs Tamora to death. Then, in implausibly rapid succession, Saturninus kills Titus and is himself killed, by Lucius, who, as the new emperor, is left to bury the dead, condemn Aaron, and 'To heal Rome's woes and wipe away her woe'.

The play's presentation of physical horror can easily seem ludicrous. There are strange disjunctions between language and acting. Marcus, seeing his niece 'with her hands cut off, and her tongue cut out, and ravished', delivers nearly fifty lines of beautifully modulated blank verse instead of calling for help; Titus, after Aaron has, at his own request, cut off his hand, shows no more emotion than if he had taken off a glove. But since the middle of the 20th century several productions, some of them relating the play to barbarism within contemporary society, have shown that its ritualistic tableaux of suffering and grief can be profoundly moving, and that the role of Titus affords opportunities for great heroic acting.

Even less conventionally historical is the romantic tragedy of *Romeo and Juliet*, based on a long poem, *The Tragical History of Romeus and Juliet*, published in 1562 and written by the short-lived Arthur Brooke, who died at sea in 1563. Shakespeare's play must have seemed daringly original to its early audiences. Richly romantic, exuberant in verbal inventiveness, it is nevertheless also highly patterned both in overall structure and in verbal detail. Public strife between the lovers' families, demonstrated in the conflict between their servants in the opening scene, is counterbalanced by the lovers' private communion; their first conversation, intimate though it is, takes the form of a shared sonnet. The Prince of Verona, the civic governor, has a counterpart in Friar Lawrence, the personal confessor. Romeo's confidant, Mercutio, is matched by Juliet's, her Nurse. Their characters are richly delineated in part through Shakespeare's verbal virtuosity but they too are part of the overall pattern, each failing one of the lovers in understanding, pushing them into tragic isolation.

Attitudes to sex and love are patterned too: the servants' dirty jokes in the opening scene, the Nurse's earthy sexuality, and Mercutio's higher-class bawdy give us sex without love, Romeo's Petrarchan passion for the unseen Rosaline gives us love without sex, but when true love blossoms Juliet looks forward to its consummation with full acknowledgement of sexuality:

> Come, civil night,
> Thou sober-suited matron all in black,
> And learn me how to lose a winning match
> Played for a pair of stainless maidenhoods. (3.2.10–13)

The lovers are destroyed by the world of external reality in which the senseless family feud, a symbol of misunderstanding, of failures in human communication, destroys the most precious representatives of their families. Romeo and Juliet had achieved understanding and risked—and in a sense lost—all for love. In this sense comedy is banished from the play's ending. But out of their suffering comes a hard-won reconciliation. As in some of Shakespeare's later comedies, such as *The Winter's Tale* and *The Tempest*, the union of lovers accompanies the healing of breaches among members of the older generation: but here, the lovers are dead.

Richard II, *Henry IV*, and *Henry V*

After his sequence of history plays about Henry VI and Richard III, often referred to as the first tetralogy, Shakespeare mined English history again to reshape events of the past into dramatic form in another sequence of four interrelated plays that display a far broader spectrum of dramatic styles.

Richard II tells the beginning of the story whose end had been staged in *Richard III*: Bolingbroke's usurpation of the throne from Richard II had set in train the entire series of events that are finally expiated only in the union of the houses of York and Lancaster celebrated in the last speech of *Richard III*. Again the focus is firmly on a single character, but Richard II is far more introverted and morally ambiguous than Richard III.

Though this play's narrative flows directly into the next in the sequence, *Henry IV, Part One*, both its dramatic mode and its linguistic style are so different from the later plays that it seems clear that Shakespeare did not conceive them as a sequence. Every character in *Richard II*—even the gardeners who compare the state of England under Richard to a neglected garden 'swarming with caterpillars' (3.4.48)—speaks entirely in patterned verse; Shakespeare forgoes stylistic variety in favour of an intense, plangent lyricism that is especially well suited to the introverted, self-pitying King. Initially he is unsympathetic, frivolous, and irresponsible: having banished Mowbray and Bolingbroke in the scene of the lists, he behaves callously to Bolingbroke's father, John of Gaunt, whose warnings against his unkingly conduct in the eloquent 'This royal throne of kings' speech (2.1.31–68) he ignores, and after his death confiscates his property with no regard for Bolingbroke's rights. During Richard's Irish campaign Bolingbroke returns from exile and gains support in his efforts to claim his due rights.

As the balance of power shifts Richard becomes more sympathetic, eloquent in his laments. When he abdicates, the slow transference of power is brought about in a scene of lyrical expansiveness, and he becomes pitiable as he is led to prison while his Queen is banished to France. The self-exploration that helps to draw us to him climaxes in his poignant prison soliloquy shortly before he is murdered. Finally Bolingbroke, now King Henry IV, plans a penitential pilgrimage to the Holy Land.

Some three years later, Shakespeare turned the events of the reign of King Henry IV into what turned out to be two plays—*Henry IV, Parts One and Two*—followed by their natural sequel, *Henry V*.

At the opening of *Henry IV, Part One* Henry, haunted by guilt and anguished by both national and filial rebellion, laments the fact that state affairs have aborted his planned pilgrimage. We had heard in *Richard II* of his dissatisfaction with Hal; this play is to show how Hal gradually, and with setbacks, redeems himself in his father's eyes. Shakespeare structures the play on the rivalry between Hal and Hotspur, the honour-hungry offspring of the King's opponent the Earl of Northumberland, making them both roughly the same age even though, historically, Hal was twenty-three years younger. The climax of their opposition comes when Hal kills Hotspur at the Battle of Shrewsbury. The play's patterning is subtle. Rebellion on a national level led by Worcester, Glyndŵr, and Hotspur is counterpointed with Hal's personal rebellion against the constraints imposed by his princely status.

In both plays Shakespeare threads through the historical action a fully developed sequence of invented scenes which move history into the theatrical and imaginative realms of comedy by introducing the character of Sir John Falstaff who, although he has his origins in the historical Sir John Oldcastle, later Lord Cobham (and bore this name until the play was censored before publication as the result of objections from the current holder of the title), so far transcends his ostensible model that he has come to be regarded as one of the greatest comic creations of all time. In *Henry IV, Part One* he serves as the deflator of Hotspur's neurotic obsession with honour and as a kind of substitute father for Prince Hal; in *Part Two*, older and more melancholy, he both focuses the play's poetic concern with the ravages of time and serves as a measure of the way in which the Prince has to compromise his human feelings in taking on the responsibilities and duties of kingship.

The journey from Hal's first soliloquy, beginning 'I know you all, and will a while uphold | The unyoked humour of your idleness' (*1 Henry IV*, 1.2.192–3) to his 'I know you not old man. Fall to thy prayers. | How ill white hairs becomes a fool and jester!' (*2 Henry IV*, 5.5.46) as, newly enthroned, he dissociates himself from his old friend and companion at the end of the second play in the series is poignant and troubling.

At the start of *Henry IV, Part Two* Hal seems to have returned to his former ways. Uncharacteristically, Shakespeare repeats the earlier play's pattern of paternal reproach, filial repentance, and reconciliation, possibly because of initial uncertainty about whether to treat Henry IV's reign in one play or two. But *Part Two*, darker and more disturbing than *Part One*, brings to the surface moral issues only latent in the earlier play. Even there Falstaff at his most contemptible, stabbing Hotspur's corpse and taking credit for killing him, was juxtaposed with Hal at his most heroic—and forgiving. Here, though we may temporarily condone Falstaff's callous misuse of his powers of conscription and his exploitation of Justice Shallow in the autumnally beautiful scenes set in a Gloucestershire orchard, his self-exculpations are less disarming. In the great tavern scene (2.4) his amorous exchanges with the prostitute Doll Tearsheet are poignant rather than funny, overshadowed by impotence and fear of death.

But Shakespeare does not encourage moral complacency. He presents Mistress Quickly and even Doll in ways that show his delight in normal human instincts along with awareness that they may get dangerously out of control. Hal's brother Prince John may have right on his side but the trick by which he betrays the rebels is distasteful; we can warm to Falstaff's condemnation of the 'sober-blooded boy'. The darker side of tavern life is savagely evident in the tiny scene in which Quickly and Doll are dragged on stage for punishment by law officers—'the man is dead that you and Pistol beat amongst you' (5.4.16–17). This scene is strategically placed straight before Hal's processional entrance as the newly crowned king and his dismissal of Falstaff, helping us to see the need for its unsentimental harshness.

In *Henry V* Shakespeare brings history close to comic form, climaxing the sequence with Henry's victory over the French and his marriage to their Princess which will unite realms as well as hearts.

From the civil broils of the earlier plays he turns to portray a country united in war against France. There is more glory in such a war, and this play, more extrovert than its predecessors, is famous—or notorious—as a celebration of patriotism. Henry's speeches before the battle of Harfleur—'Once more unto the breach, dear friends, once more, | Or close the wall up with our English dead'—and that of Agincourt—the 'St Crispin's day' speech celebrating 'We few, we happy few, we band of brothers'—have become the most admired pieces of war rhetoric in English.

But the horrors of war are not shirked. The goal of war is peace, and the play suggests that inward peace of conscience is necessary in a king who seeks national peace. Henry shows concern about the justice of his actions. More than once we are reminded of his 'wilder days'. The transition from 'madcap prince' to the 'mirror of all Christian kings' involves loss. Falstaff, we learn in a speech from Mistress Quickly of elegiac and characterful beauty that combines pathos with humour in a uniquely Shakespearian manner, has died: 'the king has killed his heart.' But Henry has accepted the responsibilities of kingship and talks of them, and of its hollow rewards, in a speech that recalls one by his father (*2 Henry IV*, 3.1-31) and anticipates (historically) one by his son (*The True Tragedy*, 2.5.1-54, quoted in part above). 'The King is but a man' (4.1.103), and this one moves among his fellow soldiers with an openness unimaginable in Richard II and quite different from his father's condescending 'courtship to the common people' (*Richard II*, 1.4.24). His success in battle expiates the guilt of his inheritance. He has become the 'star of England' (final Chorus, 6). If in the process he has made decisions that have harsh consequences, that, Shakespeare implies, is the price of political success.

Throughout this play our reactions are guided by the Chorus who speaks eloquently before each act and at the end, in the author's own person, in the form of a sonnet which rounds off the entire sequence of eight plays:

Thus far with rough and all-unable pen
    Our bending author hath pursued the story,
In little room confining mighty men,
    Mangling by starts the full course of their glory.
Small time, but in that small most greatly lived
    This star of England. Fortune made his sword,
By which the world's best garden he achieved,
    And of it left his son imperial lord.
Henry the Sixth, in infant bands crowned king
    Of France and England, did this king succeed,
Whose state so many had the managing
    That they lost France and made his England bleed,
Which oft our stage hath shown—and, for their sake,
In your fair minds let this acceptance take.

Edward III and *King John*

While Shakespeare was still a freelance writer he appears to have
contributed to *Edward III*, a jingoistic drama published in 1596
but probably written in 1594 and not included in the First Folio.
Edward was Richard II's grandfather; this play may have given
Shakespeare the idea of writing his own plays about the dynasty.
His contribution includes scenes in which the King, who has
fallen in love with the virtuous (and married) Countess of
Salisbury, expresses his passion in attractively written verse
recalling that of *The Two Gentlemen of Verona*.

More substantially, probably about 1596 he also wrote a one-off
play about an earlier period of English history, *King John*,
portraying a conflict in which neither side is right. John knows
that his claim to the throne is weak. The French King Philip
withdraws his support of the rival claimant, the young Prince
Arthur, when John offers to make an advantageous match
between his niece and the French Dauphin. Both sides put
selfishness, scheming, and personal greed—'commodity'
(2.1.575)—before the common good. Shakespeare treats the

situation ironically, in for instance the scene (2.1) before Angiers in which the blood of both sides is wasted because neither has won. There is a farcical element in the impasse and in John's acquiescence in the suggestion that the opposing armies should

> lay this Angiers even with the ground,
> Then after fight who shall be king of it. (2.1.399–400)

In the first part of the play the Bastard, Philip Faulconbridge, acts as an ironic commentator. But grief is important, too. Arthur's mother, Queen Constance, speaks powerfully of suffering and loss, and the boy's threatened blinding and his death form an emotional focus. The discovery of his corpse turns the Bastard from an ironic commentator to an involved participant, committed to humanity and his country's welfare. He ends the play with the lines

> This England never did, nor ever shall,
> Lie at the proud foot of a conqueror,
> But when it first did help to wound itself . . .
> Come the three corners of the world in arms,
>   And we shall shock them. Nought shall make us rue,
>   If England to itself do rest but true.

Chapter 5
Shakespeare and comic form

Early comedies

Close on half of Shakespeare's plays, extending from the beginning to the end of his career, are written in comic form though they play a wide range of variations on it. The five earliest are the lightest in tone. *The Two Gentlemen of Verona*, possibly his first play, has as its central theme a commonplace Renaissance debating topic, the relative claims of friendship and love. This is bodied forth in the plot by which the comradeship of two young men, Proteus and Valentine, comes under pressure when Proteus falls for Silvia, to whom his friend is engaged. The tale builds to a melodramatic and underwritten climax in which Proteus threatens to rape Silvia, whereupon Valentine implausibly displays the intensity of his friendship by offering to hand Silvia over to him: 'All that was mine in Silvia I give thee' (5.4.83).

The action is carried forward in a series of short scenes, many of them sketchily constructed in the form of soliloquies and duologues, some of which are commented upon by one or two other characters. But the verse often has a delightful lyricism which relates it to the sort of poetry that Shakespeare had read in his youth in anthologies such as *Tottel's Miscellany* (see Chapter 1), and the prose spoken by the servants is shaped with elegant artifice. Comedy and pathos come together in the ironies

that play around Julia in the pageboy disguise in which she
follows Proteus. We hear them in her little duologue with the Host
of an inn as, unseen by Proteus, she overhears his offering of the
serenade:

HOST	How now, are you sadder than you were before? How do you, man? The music likes you not.
JULIA	You mistake. The musician likes me not.
HOST	Why, my pretty youth?
JULIA	He plays false, father.
HOST	How, out of tune on the strings?
JULIA	Not so, but yet so false that he grieves my very heart-strings.
HOST	You have a quick ear.
JULIA	Ay, I would I were deaf. It makes me have a slow heart.
HOST	I perceive you delight not in music.
JULIA	Not a whit when it jars so.
HOST	Hark what fine change is in the music.
JULIA	Ay, that 'change' is the spite.
HOST	You would have them always play but one thing?
JULIA	I would always have one play but one thing. (4.2.53–69)

The Two Gentlemen of Verona is a kind of seedbed of features that
Shakespeare will use and develop in later comedies. Julia and her
maid Lucetta jest about her suitors as Portia and Nerissa will do in
The Merchant of Venice. Julia disguises herself as a boy in order to
follow the man she loves, as will Rosalind in *As You Like It*, Viola
in *Twelfth Night*, and Innogen in *Cymbeline*. Proteus' guilt over
the conflict between duty to his friend and his desire for Silvia
anticipates so serious a situation as the anguish of Angelo in
Measure for Measure when he experiences lust for Isabella.

Shakespeare places alongside the main action a series of episodes
(too sketchy to be called subplots) in which the men's servants,
Speed and Lance, comment both directly and obliquely on their
masters' faults and follies; they are the first in the long line of
Shakespeare's comic servants, fools, and clowns extending right to

the end of his career in Trinculo and Stefano in *The Tempest*. But never again did he give a significant role to a live animal (except just possibly with the bear that pursues Antigonus to his death in *The Winter's Tale*) even though Lance's dog Crab is a source of some of the play's most entertaining (as well as thematically appropriate) episodes.

Though *The Taming of the Shrew* is also set in Italy, and portrays character types deriving from commedia dell'arte, it draws more clearly on the robust traditions of earlier 16th century English farce. Shakespeare cleverly juxtaposes the emptily conventional love affair between Lucentio and Bianca with the greater emotional reality of that between Petruccio and Katherine, whose scenes crackle with wit and show developing self-awareness between both of them. Some of the liveliest and most artistically patterned writing comes in the prose speeches of comic characters such as Biondello, in his account of Petruccio on his way to the marriage (3.2.64–73), and Grumio in his description of Kate's journey to Petruccio's house (3.3.64–75). The Christopher Sly framework, which includes some of the play's finest verse, is rounded off only in the different but related play *The Taming of a Shrew* which was printed in 1594 and probably derives from a version of Shakespeare's play different from that printed in the Folio. The sting is taken out of Kate's submission to her new husband, which embarrasses many modern interpreters, if the play's main action is seen as a wish-fulfilment of Sly's turbulent relationship with his own wife.

Occasionally, especially early in his career, Shakespeare reworked a play that already existed, turning it into a creation of his own. The clearest example of this is *The Comedy of Errors*. Unusually this seems to have been written, and was certainly performed, for a particular occasion, the Christmas festivities of 1594 of one of London's law schools, Gray's Inn. One of its members was the Earl of Southampton, to whom earlier that year Shakespeare had dedicated *The Rape of Lucrece* (see Chapter 2), and who may even have commissioned the play. Shakespeare chose for the occasion to adapt a classical comedy, *Menaechmi*, by the Roman dramatist Plautus, which he may well have read at school.

The Comedy of Errors is his shortest play, and the only one that calls for no music, perhaps because that could not easily have been provided at Gray's Inn. Even so it elaborates the action of *Menaechmi*, which is typical of classical drama in that it follows the convention of the three unities of action, place, and time; this means that it has a single plot taking place in a single location within a single day. Its action derives from the embarrassment and difficulties experienced by a man in search of his long-lost twin brother when various people well known to that twin—including his wife, his mistress, and his father—mistake the one for the other.

Shakespeare brilliantly increases the possibilities, even the inevitability, of comic confusion by giving the brothers—both confusingly called Antipholus—twin servants who also have identical names—Dromio—and who also have been separated since infancy. The brothers are visiting Ephesus, and whereas in Plautus there is no one whom the visiting brother, Antipholus of Syracuse, is likely to take for anyone else, in Shakespeare he too can be wrong, about the servants, both of them confusingly (and improbably) named Dromio. So every character knows, and may encounter, either a twin master or a twin servant or both, and thus is liable to error, except the Abbess who appears only in the final scene; the fact that she is not liable to error suits her function of resolving the complexities of the action. So Shakespeare's doubling of Plautus' twins enhances the play's witty intellectuality. Also he relaxes the action by building in a number of set pieces, notably the comic catechism (3.2.71–152) in which Dromio of Syracuse describes to his master the fat kitchen wench—'She is spherical, like a globe'—who has designs on him.

If this were all, the play would be a clever though rather heartless farce. But it is typical of Shakespeare that he broadens the play's emotional range by enclosing the farcical action within a serious framework, which itself derives from another classical story, one that he was to use again towards the end of his career in *Pericles*.

This framing action tells the story of Egeon, father of the twin masters, who is visiting Ephesus in search of his lost sons and whom the Duke of Ephesus condemns to die unless he can find someone to pay his debts before the end of the single day in which the action takes place. Egeon is a still centre to the play. In the final scene his distress when he believes that the son whom he has brought up from birth rejects him provides the catalyst for a dramatic climax in which, for the first time in Shakespeare's career, laughter and pathos intermingle in a manner that has come to be thought of as typical of Shakespearian comedy.

The first of Shakespeare's plays to have a plot spun entirely from his own imagination is *Love's Labour's Lost*, a highly patterned comedy clearly based on a structure of ideas. The King of Navarre and his three courtiers Biron, Longueville, and Dumaine band together in a pact to forswear worldly pleasures, including female company, for three years and to devote themselves to study. They have reckoned without the imminent arrival on a diplomatic mission of the Princess of France with, predictably, three ladies, Rosaline, Maria, and Catherine. Much comedy arises from the men's efforts to disguise from one another the fact that they are falling in love, and from the ladies' practical joke in exchanging identities when, disguised as Russians, the men come to woo them with an entertainment.

Shakespeare counterpoints the main action with events involving characters based in part, as in *The Taming of the Shrew*, on the type figures of commedia dell'arte who reflect aspects of the lords' personalities. The sterility of the path they are treading is polarized in the arid intellectualities of the pedantic schoolmaster Holofernes, seen always in the company of his sidekick the curate Sir Nathaniel ('Sir' is a courtesy title for a clergyman, not a token of knighthood). The dangers that lie in the other direction are pointed by the amoral antics of Costard, an amiable, unsophisticated yokel, and his girl friend Jaquenetta. Don Adriano de Armado, 'a refinèd traveller of Spain', who lusts after Jaquenetta, is a pompous and affected ass who precipitates the play's climax by getting her pregnant.

Much of the comedy of this play derives from fulfilment of the audience's expectations, especially in the brilliantly patterned scene in which, one by one, the men admit that they have fallen in love, climaxing in Biron's eloquent paean in praise of love in which he admits that they can fulfil themselves only by breaking their oaths:

> It is religion to be thus forsworn,
> For charity itself fulfils the law,
> And who can sever love from charity? (4.3.339–41)

When the play came to be printed from Shakespeare's manuscript this speech accidentally included both unrevised and revised versions of a number of lines, providing an exceptional opportunity to see Shakespeare at work (Figure 7).

The play's language, full of brilliantly sophisticated and at times extremely bawdy wordplay—which makes it easier to see than to read—shows Shakespeare's verbal skills at their youthful best. But it is flecked through with intimations of mortality which break surface in the final scene at the climax of the comic action when, in a total and daring violation of expectation, Mercadé enters to bring news of the Princess's father's death. His very appearance on the crowded scene—he is always dressed in black—is enough. The most important statement of this extremely verbal play is communicated without words. The closing episode, as the courtly lovers slowly readjust to the sombre situation, represents Shakespeare's most daring experiment with comic form.

7. *Love's Labour's Lost*: 4.3: an opening from the first Quarto (1598). The passage beginning 'And where that you haue vowd to studie . . .' is a first draft, accidentally included, of the passage beginning 'O we haue made a Vow to studie . . .'.

Shakespeare also invented the overall plot of *A Midsummer Night's Dream*, though it draws on a variety of sources from both folklore and literature including Chaucer's *Knight's Tale* both for the enveloping action involving Theseus, Duke of Athens, and Hippolyta as they prepare for their marriage, and for the love story of Hermia and Lysander. He counterpoints these with the story of the initially broken marriage of the fairy King and Queen, Oberon and Titania, and with the episodes in which a group of workmen, or mechanicals, who seem far more likely to have come from his native Warwickshire than from ancient Athens, prepare and eventually perform for the Duke's wedding an entertainment based on the tale of Pyramus and Thisbe from Ovid's *Metamorphoses*. A mischievous puck, or pixie, Robin Goodfellow,

who serves Oberon, spans the worlds of the play almost literally—
he says he can 'put a girdle round about the earth in forty
minutes'—delighting in the lovers' misfortunes and interfering in
the workmen's rehearsals.

The play is a kind of comic counterpart to the tragedy of *Romeo
and Juliet*, which seems either to be parodied or foreshadowed in
the mock tragedy of Pyramus and Thisbe. It is valued for the
fantasy of its comedy, the brilliant lyricism of its depiction of the
fairy world, its masterly deployment of a wide range of poetic
forms, the humanity as well as the broad comedy of its depiction
of the efforts of the workmen to please their rulers (and in the
process to earn 'sixpence a day' for their leader), and the broadly
parodic fun deriving from the comic failure of the entertainment
that they rehearse and disastrously perform for the multiple
weddings of the final scene.

All this has served to make this the most popular of Shakespeare's
plays among young people. (I sometimes allow myself to toy in
unscholarly fashion with the thought that Shakespeare might have
had his own children in mind as he wrote it—they would have
been about 11 and 13 years old.) But it is also, along with *The
Tempest*, the play in which Shakespeare is most clearly, however
playfully, concerned with his art, the powers of imagination
(discussed at length in Theseus's speech and, no less importantly,
Hippolyta's response to it, 5.1.1–29), the creative capacity of the
artist, and the imaginary interplay between the dramatist, his
actors, and his audience. Most of Shakespeare's comedies end not,
as is often said, with marriage but with marriage expected or
deferred. This one ends with celebration not of one but of three
marriages, and with the fairies' benediction on them all.

Later comedies for the Lord Chamberlain's Men

In all the comedies that I have discussed so far—even *Love's
Labour's Lost*—all the characters share in their more or less

harmonious endings. But in the five that follow Shakespeare introduces an antagonist who must be expelled before the play can end happily.

The main plot of *The Merchant of Venice* comes from an Italian story published in 1558 that had not been translated when Shakespeare wrote the play; presumably he read it in Italian. (Portia makes fun of her English suitor because he 'has neither Latin, French, nor Italian' (1.2.66–7); I like to think that Shakespeare would not have written this if he had been similarly unlettered.) He transforms a rather sordid tale of a widow who challenges suitors to seduce her on pain of losing their wealth, and who thwarts them by drugging their wine, into the romantic plot of the wealthy and beautiful maiden Portia bound by her father's will to accept only the suitor who makes the right choice among caskets of gold, silver, and lead. Belmont—'beautiful mountain'— where she lives, is set against the commercial world of Venice where her preferred suitor, Bassanio, needs to borrow money from his friend Antonio to cover his wooing expenses. Once more Shakespeare takes up the theme of the conflict between friendship and love, when Antonio enters into a 'merry bond' with the Jewish moneylender Shylock by which he will forfeit a pound of flesh 'to be cut off and taken | In what part of your body pleaseth me' (1.3.149–50) if he cannot repay the debt he enters into on his friend's behalf. In the trial scene, a masterpiece of dramatic construction, Shakespeare builds the tension to a high pitch in which, against expectation, Antonio is required to fulfil the bond and to offer his breast to Shylock's knife. He is saved only by a last-minute intervention by Portia.

Antonio's love for Bassanio is so strong that their relationship is often regarded as homoerotic. But the central interpretative problem of the play lies in the portrayal of Shylock. Though he is vindictive, he is true to his own code of conduct. Shakespeare gives him powerful speeches of self-defence—'Hath not a Jew eyes . . .'—and makes the Christians open to criticism—'You have

among you many a purchased slave . . .' (4.1.89). The role can
become tragic in impact, and the play has often been regarded as
anti-Semitic. Forcibly stripped of his wealth, Shylock leaves the
courtroom a broken man. The last act modulates from romantic
lyricism to high comedy while sustaining the play's deeper concern
with true and false values.

There is a legend that Shakespeare wrote *The Merry Wives of
Windsor* because Queen Elizabeth wanted to see 'Sir John
[Falstaff] in love'. It is unusual for Shakespeare in several ways: it
is (except for the Induction to *The Taming of the Shrew*) his only
comedy set in England; it contains a higher proportion of prose to
verse than any other of his plays; and except for a few passing
references to the time of Henry IV there is nothing to suggest that
the action takes place before Shakespeare's time. Full of details
that would have been familiar to its early audiences, it contains
Shakespeare's most extended topical reference, the lines (often
omitted in modern performance) in the last act which pay an
extended compliment to Queen Elizabeth and which link the play
with ceremonies held at Windsor Castle in connection with the
Order of the Garter, the highest order of knighthood, which was
(and is) in the Queen's gift. It seems clear that the play was
originally written for a special occasion which we cannot identify.

Critics sometimes grumble that Falstaff here is not the man he
was in the history plays; he might have had a better press if
Shakespeare had given him a different name. But he speaks richly
characterful prose, racy and eminently actable. After he has been
tumbled into the Thames in a laundry basket:

> . . . you may know by my size that I have a kind of alacrity in
> sinking. If the bottom were as deep as hell, I should down. I had
> been drowned, but that the shore was shelvy and shallow—a death
> that I abhor, for the water swells a man, and what a thing should I
> have been when I had been swelled! By the Lord, a mountain of
> mummy [dead flesh]! (3.5.11–17)

The play has excellent comic episodes such as that in which the wives read to each other the love letter that Falstaff has sent to each of them simultaneously (2.1), the one involving a laundry basket in which Falstaff hides (3.3), and the later one (4.2) in which he turns out not to be in the basket after all. The unjustified jealousy of Master Ford, husband of one of the wives, is a source of farcical comedy, but after the complex midnight scene in which Falstaff—the antagonist in this play—is frightened out of his lechery, all ends in forgiveness and love.

Don John, the antagonist in *Much Ado About Nothing*, set in Sicily, is a two-dimensional villain. In the main plot, he maliciously deceives the young soldier Claudio into believing that his fiancée, Hero, has taken a lover on the eve of their marriage. He cruelly repudiates her at the altar in a plot that Shakespeare reworked from a traditional tale.

As in *The Taming of the Shrew*, Shakespeare offsets the plot involving a superficially romantic pair of lovers, written mostly in verse, with one about an apparently unromantic relationship, that between Beatrice and Benedick, conducted mainly in prose, whose friends trick them into falling in love with one another in cleverly devised scenes of situation comedy. Their edgy relationship as they spar verbally, often with psychologically revealing nuances, recalls that of Katherine and Petruccio in *The Taming of the Shrew*. Beatrice speaks verse, in the form of a truncated sonnet, for the first time when she emerges from hiding after hearing her friends say that Benedick loves her:

> What fire is in mine ears? Can this be true?
>> Stand I condemned for pride and scorn so much?
> Contempt, farewell; and maiden pride, adieu.
>> No glory lies behind the back of such.
> And, Benedick, love on. I will requite thee,
>> Taming my wild heart to thy loving hand. (3.1.107–12)

It is a speech of self-discovery which can become the psychological heart of the role.

The prose episode (4.1.258–335) in which Beatrice and Benedick acknowledge their love for one another at the end of the scene in which Claudio caddishly rejects Hero at the altar touches deeper chords of emotion than anything in what is technically the main plot. Hero's apparent death, anticipating that of Hermione in *The Winter's Tale*, brings the play close to the genre of tragicomedy. Don John's villainy is eventually brought to light by the bumbling but well-intentioned incompetence of the very English constable Dogberry, a role written for Will Kemp (see Chapter 2), and his fellow watchmen.

At various points of his career and in a variety of plays from *The Two Gentlemen of Verona* onwards Shakespeare plays variations on the conventions of pastoral literature that go back to ancient times—the idea that the countryside is a place where shepherds and shepherdesses lead lives of unhurried ease in contrast with the bustle and corruption of the city and the court. The most pastoral of all his plays is *As You Like It*, adapted from Thomas Lodge's popular *Rosalynde* (1590), which makes it especially suited to outdoor performance. It has two antagonists: the tyrannical usurper Duke Frederick, in whose court the action begins, and the villainous Oliver, elder brother of the hero Orlando, who however will undergo a sudden conversion when, experiencing the beneficial influence of country life, he falls in love.

Shakespeare repeats the patterning of *Love's Labour's Lost* but makes it more subtle by placing Silvius, who in Petrarchan fashion loves the apparently unattainable Phoebe, on one side of the romantic hero and heroine Orlando and Rosalind, and on the other side the jester Touchstone and his woman Audrey, with whom his 'loving voyage | Is but for two months victualled' (5.4.189–90). He adds as detached commentator the wryly acerbic and resolutely unattached Jaques, to whom he gives the famous 'ages of man' speech (2.7.139–66).

Once Rosalind, banished from her uncle Duke Frederick's court, and her cousin Celia have reached the forest of Ardenne disguised as Ganymede and Aliena Shakespeare virtually suspends plot in favour of a succession of scintillating conversations which, though often lyrically poetic, are written mainly in prose. Like Julia in *The Two Gentlemen of Verona*, Rosalind spends most of the play disguised as a boy, Ganymede, the name of one of Jove's cup-bearers often used in Shakespeare's time of a boy-lover. Her/his mock-marriage to Orlando (4.1.116–90) thus has especially strong homoerotic overtones which would have been enhanced when the role was played by a boy. Shakespeare incorporates into his text many elements of popular entertainment—songs including 'It was a lover and his lass' (5.3.15–38), dances, comic set pieces such as Touchstone's disquisition on lying (5.3.68–101), and, anticipating the climaxes of his final romances, his first theophany—the appearance of a god—Hymen, in the final episode, which brings the action to a poetically serious conclusion.

The great sequence of Shakespeare's romantic comedies culminates in *Twelfth Night*, acted in 1602 at a feast in the Middle Temple, a law school like Gray's Inn, and probably written soon after *Hamlet*. The main plot romanticizes and makes less sexually explicit a story printed in 1581 in a book called *Riche's Farewell to Military Profession*. As in *The Comedy of Errors*, the action centres on twins—though this time only one pair. Courtship is central to the plot. The Countess Olivia is wooed by Duke Orsino, Sir Andrew Aguecheek, and even by her steward Malvolio, and Olivia woos the girl Viola in her disguise as a boy and later, when the disguise has been penetrated, Viola's brother Sebastian. Clearly there is much room for gender confusion, and the scene (2.4) between Orsino and the disguised Viola in which she comes close to confessing love for him has the same kind of potential for homoerotic interpretation as the mock-marriage of Orlando and Rosalind/Ganymede in *As You Like It*.

Twelfth Night is concerned with other sorts of love and friendship too: with the affection amounting to desire (3.3.4) of the sea-captain Antonio for Viola's brother Sebastian; with the love of brother and sister in Viola and Sebastian which climaxes in the rapt wonder of their antiphon of reunion (5.5.1.224–56), when each discovers the other has survived the play's opening shipwreck; and, on other levels, the self-love of Malvolio and the mercenary relationship of Olivia's uncle Sir Toby Belch and his foolish friend Sir Andrew Aguecheek.

In this play the comic antagonist is Malvolio (the name means 'ill-wisher') who—like Falstaff in *The Merry Wives of Windsor*—is also its butt, provoker of much of the play's comedy in the trick played upon him to make him believe that his mistress loves him but also (like another antagonist, Shylock) a victim who can arouse sympathy even though he expels himself from the play's happy ending with the cry of 'I'll be revenged on the whole pack of you' (5.1.374). And constantly mediating between the audience and the world of the play is the melancholy jester Feste, with his bitter-sweet songs of the wind and the rain and 'Come away death', his wry jests, and his air of knowing everyone in the play better than they know themselves.

Chapter 6
Return to tragedy

Hamlet, Othello, King Lear, and *Macbeth*

It is a tribute to the playgoers of the Globe that Shakespeare's longest play, one of the most complex and intellectually ambitious ever written, was, as numerous early allusions show, also one of his most popular. *Hamlet*, based on a Scandinavian folk-tale, is skilfully contrived to appeal on many levels at once. Many of its elements would have been familiar to its early audiences. It offers such well-tried theatrical devices as a ghost, a play within the play, a mad scene, a duel, and several dramatic deaths. Shakespeare's mastery of a wide variety of linguistic skills enables him to create distinctive styles with which to individualize such diverse characters as Claudius, the Ghost, Polonius, the gravedigger, and Osric. Emotionally too the range is wide. This is Shakespeare's most humorous tragedy, but the comedy is not incidental. Polonius' verbal deviousness and Osric's affected circumlocutions, comic in themselves, are among the many barriers to honest communication which intensify Hamlet's dilemma. The gravedigger's phlegmatic humour is an essential element in his contemplation of death. And his wit has both a princely elegance that adds to the sense of waste evoked by his destruction and a savage intellectuality that defines his isolation from those around him and serves as a weapon against hypocrisy and deception.

Hamlet is a raw nerve in the court of Denmark, disconcertingly liable to make the instinctive rather than the expected response. This cuts him off from his fellows but puts him into a position of peculiar intimacy with the audience. The language of his soliloquies presents us not with conclusions but with the very processes of his thinking.

> That it should come to this—
> But two months dead—nay, not so much, not two—
> So excellent a king, that was to this
> Hyperion to a satyr, so loving to my mother
> That he might not beteem the winds of heaven
> Visit her face too roughly! Heaven and earth,
> Must I remember? Why, she would hang on him
> As if increase of appetite had grown
> By what it fed on, and yet within a month—
> Let me not think on't; frailty, thy name is woman—
> A little month, or ere those shoes were old
> With which she followed my poor father's body,
> Like Niobe, all tears, why she, even she—
> O, God, a beast that wants discourse of reason
> Would have mourned longer!—married with mine uncle,
> My father's brother, but no more like my father
> Than I to Hercules; within a month,
> Ere yet the salt of most unrighteous tears
> Had left the flushing of her gallèd eyes,
> She married. O most wicked speed, to post
> With such dexterity to incestuous sheets!
> It is not, nor it cannot come to good.
> But break, my heart, for I must hold my tongue. (1.2.137–59)

The anguish that it causes Hamlet to think of his mother's over-hasty marriage is conveyed as much by the tortured syntax as by direct statement; we share his difficulty as he tries—and fails—to assimilate these unwelcome facts to his consciousness, seeking to bring under emotional control the discordant elements of his disrupted universe: his love of his mother combined with disgust at her over-hasty marriage to the uncle whom he loathes, and the disillusion with womankind that this has provoked in him. The short exclamations interrupting the sentence structure point his horror: the rhythms of ordinary speech within the verse give immediacy to the contrasts in phrases such as 'Hyperion to a satyr' and 'Than I to Hercules'; and the concreteness of the imagery betrays the unwelcome nature of the facts that it expresses: his mother's haste to remarry 'or ere those shoes were old | With which she followed my poor father's body'—it is as if only by concentrating on the matter-of-fact, physical aspects of the scene can he bear to contemplate it, or bring it within his belief. He ends on a note of utter helplessness: he alone sees the truth; he knows that his mother's actions, which both he and she see as evil, must bring forth evil; but he, the only emotionally honest person there, cannot express his emotion—except to us, the audience. Never before had dramatic language so vividly revealed 'the quick forge and working-house of thought' (*Henry V*, Chorus to Act 5, l. 23).

Hamlet's progress through the play is a dual exploration of outer and inner worlds. The Ghost's command requires him to discover the truth about those who surround him; it also leads him to intense self-questioning about his attitudes to life and especially to death. During this process he both undergoes and inflicts suffering. He causes mental anguish to his mother and to Ophelia, for whose death he is indirectly responsible. He kills Polonius and engineers the deaths of Rosencrantz and Guildenstern. He arrives finally at the truth about the world about him.

Whether he also reaches a state of self-knowledge and acceptance is a matter of interpretation. Does he die in a state of fatalistic submission to worldly values, or of spiritual grace reflecting both personal integrity and an acknowledgement of human responsibility? We share in his self-questioning.

Two or three years later Shakespeare wrote *Othello*, a tragedy based not on history or legend but on a sordid tale by Giraldi Cinthio (1504–73) which he seems to have read in the original Italian. The decision to make a Moor the hero of a tragedy was bold: traditionally—as with Aaron in *Titus Andronicus*—blackness was associated with evil.

The action, set in Venice and Cyprus, draws on a conflict between Turkey and Venice that had happened some thirty years previously. This play is a domestic tragedy in that we are invited to concentrate on its central figures as individuals rather than to see a connection between their fates and universal, elemental forces. Its hero is a servant of the state, not a ruler. It has the smallest cast of all Shakespeare's tragedies, and its most powerful scenes take place in private, not in public, culminating in a bedroom.

Whereas *Hamlet* is discursive and amplificatory, *Othello* is swift, concise, and tautly constructed. All Shakespeare's tragedies show evil at work, but here it is concentrated into a single individual. Iago is the playwright within the play, making up the plot as he goes along. The play's significance resides largely in the passions and fates of the individuals we see before us.

But Shakespeare does not present the action as a documentary imitation of reality. We are made conscious of paradox. Iago, who revels in his villainy in soliloquy to the audience, is 'honest' to everyone within the play except Roderigo. Othello's blackness joins with the traditional symbolism of black and white as a source of irony and ambiguity. The wine that makes Cassio drunk is an image of the verbal poison that Iago pours into Othello's ears—'O God', Cassio says, 'that men should put an enemy in their mouths to steal away their brains!' (3.1.283–5). The language draws attention to general concepts and stimulates us to reflect on the vagaries of human behaviour.

Iago is a rationalist. His characteristic language is a cynically reductive prose. He speaks of the act of love as a bestial coupling:

'An old black ram | Is tupping your white ewe' (1.1.88–9). Othello on the other hand is a nobly credulous idealist whose 'free and open nature' makes him think 'men honest that but seem to be so' (1.3.391–2). Shakespeare creates for him a magniloquent verse style suggestive of imagination rather than intellectuality. It is the contrast between Othello and Iago, the way that Iago drags Othello down to his own level, which forms the central dramatic action. The universality of the play lies in our consciousness of Iago's plausibility and our sympathy with Othello's insecurities, our awareness, even our fear, that inside the most loving human relationship there may lie seeds that will destroy it.

Shakespeare's determination not to court easy popularity, to pursue his internal vision with integrity even if to do so might stretch his audience's and his actors' capacities, is evident in *King Lear*, his most uncompromising play. Here he compounds a story from legendary history which had been told briefly by Holinshed and had already been used for a play of unknown authorship, which Shakespeare knew, with one from prose fiction—the plot involving the Earl of Gloucester comes from Sidney's *Arcadia*.

The interweaving of these stories is crucial to Shakespeare's design. Lear and Gloucester are both faulty, but not wicked. Lear has two evil daughters—Goneril and Regan—and one good one, Cordelia, Gloucester has a good son, Edgar, and a bad one, Edmund. Both Lear and Gloucester show bad judgement. Both men favour their evil offspring who however turn against them. Both wrong their good offspring, and suffer as a consequence. Both learn the truth before they die.

Gloucester's error and suffering are mainly physical. His evil son, Edmund, is a bastard begotten in adultery. The climax of Gloucester's suffering comes in a devastating scene when Cornwall and Regan pluck out his eyes. Lear's fault lies in his warped judgement; his suffering is primarily mental, reaching a climax in his madness after his daughters have driven him out into the storm.

Other characters relate to this patterning—the Fool tries to help Lear intellectually, Kent physically; Edmund's adulterous sexuality recalls his father's; Edgar is able to help his father both practically and spiritually. The callous, sceptical rationality of Edmund, Goneril, and Regan is opposed to the imagination and sympathy of Edgar and Cordelia.

The play's structuring around the two basic components of human life, the body and the mind, shows how concerned with fundamentals Shakespeare is in this play. He stresses the pre-Christian setting of his story, avoiding any suggestion of religious dogma. Stripped of the consolations of received religion the play gains in mystery, in the sense of life as a battle with the elements, a struggle for survival against wind and rain in a world where humanity has to compete with animal forces both within and outside itself. The mad Lear and the blind Gloucester both go through purgatory, communing with one another in a surreal scene at Dover (4.5). After this comes Lear's return to sanity and his reconciliation with Cordelia, which is also a reconciliation with life.

This might have been the end of the story, but Lear still has lessons to learn. The play ends in an assertion of the power of human love as, in a total reversal of the situation at the beginning of the play, Lear looks into the eyes of the daughter whom he had vowed never to see again. But she is dead.

Shakespeare may well have had his company's Scottish-born patron, King James, in mind when he decided to write a play about Macbeth around the time of the Gunpowder Plot. James regarded Banquo as his direct ancestor, and the play includes a scene (4.1) that relates to this. The text that has survived, printed in the First Folio, is exceptionally short and probably represents a late adaptation by Middleton.

Shakespeare treats the story, derived from Holinshed, far more freely than in his plays about English history. Even more than in

King Lear he seems to be interested rather in general ideas than in historical detail or in particularity of characterization. King Duncan is primarily a symbol of the values that Macbeth denies in murdering him. Even Banquo, initially Macbeth's companion in arms, figures mainly as a measure of the norm from which Macbeth deviates.

No less symbolical—though vivid in their evil—are the Weird Sisters who, with their incantations, spells, and grotesque rituals, suggest evil as a universal force that can be tapped and channelled by human agents:

> Come, you spirits
> That tend on mortal thoughts, unsex me here,
> And fill me from the crown to the toe top-full
> Of direst cruelty (1.4.39–42)

says Lady Macbeth when she hears that Duncan is on his way to the castle where he will be murdered. She sins through a denial of imagination, seeking to rationalize the inexplicable: 'The sleeping and the dead are but as pictures' (2.2.51–2), 'A little water clears us of this deed' (2.2.65). But her repression of natural instinct finally breaks down: her sleep-walking scene, a soliloquy unheard even by its speaker, reveals the subconscious acknowledgement in her divided being of the power of the imagination.

Macbeth's journey through the play follows the opposite trajectory, a slow death of the imagination from his initial vivid horror at the temptations that assail him to the desolation of

> Out, out, brief candle.
> Life's but a walking shadow, a poor player
> That struts and frets his hour upon the stage,
> And then is heard no more. It is a tale
> Told by an idiot, full of sound and fury,
> Signifying nothing. (5.5.22–7)

A change of direction

The Lord Chamberlain's Men had become the King's Men in 1603. Perhaps coincidentally, Shakespeare's comedies, and his work in general, took on darker tones, a new seriousness round about this time. Both *Measure for Measure* and *All's Well That Ends Well*, for instance, place their heroines in far more painful situations than those in which the central characters of the earlier comedies find themselves.

It is unfashionable, indeed it is often regarded as unscholarly, to look for reflections of an artist's life in his work. But that work comes from the mind of a person who is affected by life experiences and whose imagination responds not only to the stimuli that come from books and other works of art but also to the thoughts and emotions provoked by external events, both personal and public. In 1603 Shakespeare was approaching 40 years old. His only son had died in 1596 at the age of 11. In 1601 his father died. We have no record of how he responded to these deaths and it is fruitless to look for direct reflections of them in his work, such as suggesting that when (as in *King John*) he portrays the death of a child, or someone grieving for a dead child, he was necessarily putting into words his feelings on Hamnet's death. But in works that use fictional stories to reflect as profoundly as Shakespeare's do on the vicissitudes of human life, on what people feel in situations of extreme danger, or temptation, or ambition, or despair, or joy, or ecstasy, or grief, it is natural to suppose that the artist is drawing, however obliquely, on personal experience.

The next play after *Twelfth Night* to be written in comic form, if our chronology is correct, is *Measure for Measure*. Its very title, alluding to Jesus' teaching—'with what measure ye mete, it shall be measured to you again'—signals a play with a greater degree of moral seriousness than the comedies that had gone before. But it is not moralistic; the maxim implied by the title is explored rather than asserted. The story of a woman who, in seeking to save the life of a male relative, arouses the lust of a man in authority was not new; Shakespeare drew on an unperformed two-part play by George Whetstone, *Promos and Cassandra*, published in 1578.

The surviving text has odd features, most conspicuously that, although the setting is Vienna, the leading characters have Italian names. Shakespeare's original play seems to have been lightly adapted, with a change of setting, after he died, probably by Thomas Middleton, to make it more topical. In the Oxford *Complete Works* the play is printed in its familiar, adapted form.

Like *The Merchant of Venice*, *Measure for Measure* is much concerned with issues of justice and mercy, which it treats through the uses and abuses of power. As usual with Shakespeare it does so in an exploratory rather than a moralistic or didactic manner, representing the conflicting emotions and internal struggles of the characters rather than reflecting didactically on their situations. Angelo, deputed by the Duke to reinforce the laws of a state that has become morally lax, finds himself tempted to seduce the novice Isabella even as she pleads with him to show mercy to her brother Claudio, who has been condemned to death for premarital fornication—a sin that, incidentally, Shakespeare himself had committed. It is a severe judgement, since Claudio and his Juliet had been as close to marriage as it was possible to get, lacking only the formality of a church service.

The scenes between Angelo and Isabella are tense with excitement which reaches a climax in the prison to which the condemned Claudio has been committed. Shakespeare's capacity to imagine himself into totally opposing states of mind is apparent in the difference between the speech in which the Duke offers consolation to the condemned man—'Be absolute for death. Either death or life | Shall thereby be the sweeter'—and that in which Claudio breaks down in terror at the prospect of death:

> Ay, but to die and go we know not where;
> To lie in cold obstruction, and to rot;
> This sensible warm motion to become
> A kneaded clod, and the dilated spirit
> To bathe in fiery floods, or to reside
> In thrilling region of thick-ribbèd ice… (3.1.118–23)

Up to this point the play might be going to end as a tragedy, but the Duke averts disaster by thinking up the bed-trick by which Angelo is tricked into sleeping with Mariana, whom he had long since jilted, under the illusion that she is Isabella.

Here the play shifts from emotional realism to theatrical artifice. The main vehicle of expression turns from verse to prose, and the emotional temperature goes down as Shakespeare and the Duke between them manipulate the action to a morally dubious ending with the restoration of the supposedly dead Claudio to his sister, two forced marriages—Angelo to Mariana and the play's main comic character, Lucio, to a prostitute—and an unanswered proposal of marriage from the Duke to Isabella.

There is another bed-trick in *All's Well That Ends Well*, but here it is used to help a woman to lose her virginity, not to preserve it. Shakespeare's play, based on a story from Boccaccio's *Decameron*, tells how a dead physician's daughter, Helen, seeks to heal a sick king and demands in return the hand in marriage of a handsome young nobleman, Bertram, son of the Countess of Roussillon who has brought her up. The story might have turned out as a fairy tale, but although Helen succeeds in curing the King, who in gratitude uses his power to make Bertram marry her, he cannot force him to love her. The young man snobbishly refuses to consummate the marriage because she is only 'a poor physician's daughter'.

The play becomes a psychologically acute study in embarrassment mirrored in the bitterly comic subplot, invented by Shakespeare, of Bertram's companion, the braggart soldier Paroles, whose name signals his flashiness, and whose exposure as a coward reflects upon Bertram's behaviour. Finally, as in *Measure for Measure*, the action can be resolved only by a resurrection. Bertram thinks Helen has died, but as a consequence of another bed-trick she is pregnant by him. His sudden claim to repentance and plea for forgiveness leave much to the actor. He is likely to kneel as Isabella does in asking the Duke to pardon Angelo. But this is unlikely to make us feel that heaven has brought about a moral cure of Bertram in the way that Helen has physically cured the King, whose last words both to those on stage and to us, the audience, belie the play's title:

> All yet seems well; and if it end so meet,
> The bitter past, more welcome is the sweet.

And to us, in the conventional request for applause:

> All is well ended if this suit be won:
> That you express content . . .

Both *Measure for Measure* and *All's Well That Ends Well*, only conditionally happy in their endings, interrogate comic form, bearing witness to Shakespeare's restless imagination's refusal to repeat itself.

Chapter 7
Classical plays

As we have seen, Shakespeare's grammar-school education gave him a thorough grounding in Latin, and possibly some Greek, and in the writings of classical authors. He drew on and developed this knowledge at every stage of his career, most conspicuously in the remarkably diverse tragedies and other plays in which he dramatized Greek and Roman history.

During the seven or so years that passed between the writing of *Titus Andronicus* and his next Roman play he learned a lot. Above all he read North's translation of Plutarch (see Chapter 1) on which he draws heavily but with an unerring sense of drama in *Julius Caesar*. The play is not a one-man show. Though Caesar remains a force to be reckoned with even after he is assassinated about half way through the action, his friend Antony and the conspirators Brutus and Cassius share the dramatic limelight. Brutus, self-deluded, 'with himself at war' (1.2.46), dressing up the murder in noble but hollow words—'Let's be sacrificers, but not butchers, Caius' (2.1.166)—talks of 'waving our red weapons o'er our heads' while simultaneously crying 'Peace, freedom, and liberty!' (3.1.110–11), rhetoric that leads to the senseless and brutal murder of Cinna the poet at the climax of the play's magnificently constructed first great sweep of action.

The uses and abuses of rhetoric, with which the Romans were especially associated, becomes an implicit theme of the play. With it Cassius seduces Brutus into taking part in the murder, and into thinking murder a virtuous act. Caesar creates glory for himself by a rhetoric of action as well as words, and in the Forum scene following the assassination Shakespeare's mastery of theatrical rhetoric enables him to demonstrate the power of emotive speech to sway men in the theatre of the world, overwhelming reason by passion. We take aesthetic pleasure in the virtuosity with which Shakespeare's artistry endows Antony as he calmly, intellectually manipulates the citizens' actions. Words are important in the quarrel between Brutus and Cassius (4.2), in Antony's taunt that Brutus has tried to disguise his guilt with 'good words' (5.1.30), and in the fact that false words cause Cassius' death. Antony ends the play with fine words about Brutus—'This was the noblest Roman of them all' (5.5.67)—but are they true? Does Shakespeare end with an affirmation or an implied question? With an endorsement of the verdict of history, or a hint that history has its own rhetoric, no more to be trusted than any other of the words of men?

The most difficult of Shakespeare's plays to categorize—and one of the most demanding, though also ultimately rewarding, to read—is *Troilus and Cressida*, written some time before February 1603 when it was registered for publication with a statement that it had been played at the Globe. That statement was repeated in some copies of the quarto edition of 1609, but denied in others. In the Folio (on which the Oxford text is based) it was to have been included among the tragedies but was finally placed between the histories and the tragedies. There are big differences between the two texts, showing that at some point it was substantially revised.

It is only partly classical, deriving from George Chapman's 1598 translation of Homer and other sources for the scenes relating to the siege of Troy, but from Chaucer's *Troilus and Criseyde* for the love story. It is a highly intellectual play using an exceptionally learned vocabulary. Shakespeare is not just telling a story but using it to offer poetic exploration of complex philosophical issues. Maybe he wrote it for private performance before a specialist audience.

Its plot deals with what was regarded as the first important event in the history of the world. Great characters of antiquity—Agamemnon, Achilles, Ajax, Hector—are portrayed as all too fallibly human. Helen, whose adultery caused the Trojan War, is shown on her single appearance (3.1) as a silly sensualist. Though the tone is in many ways tragic no character rises to fully tragic stature. The most poignant figure is Troilus. Shakespeare makes us feel the sensual intensity of his passion for Cressida:

> I am giddy. Expectation whirls me round.
> Th'imaginary relish is so sweet
> That it enchants my sense. (3.216–18)

We feel too his sense of betrayal when she deserts him for Diomedes.

> If beauty have a soul, this is not she.
> If souls guide vows, if vows be sanctimonies,
> If sanctimony be the gods' delight,
> If there be rule in unity itself.
> This is not she. (5.2.141–5)

But we also see him, and other characters, as through the wrong end of a telescope, distanced, diminished. Then 'love, friendship, charity' are seen as 'subjects all | To envious and calumniating Time' (3.3.173–4). Agamemnon epitomizes part of the play's effect in his contrast between the 'extant moment' and 'what's past and what's to come', which is 'strewed with husks | And formless ruin of oblivion' (4.1.166). Thersites, the bitter professional fool, is deflating, reductive, savagely bitter. As he reduces war to its lowest level, so Cressida's uncle, Pandarus—the archetypal pander—reduces love. At the end of the play in its first version he breaks through the barrier that links past and present, suggesting a vision of all that lies between as a 'formless ruin of oblivion'. Nothing of the great events of Troy remains except a dying old pander bequeathing his diseases to the audience. This is Shakespeare's bleakest play.

But *Timon of Athens* runs it a close second, which may be why the surviving text is incomplete; editors do something to tidy it up, and theatre directors need to do more to put it into performable shape. We now know that it was one of Shakespeare's late collaborations, written with the young Thomas Middleton.

It is based mainly on a brief anecdote told by Plutarch, and divides clearly into two parts: the first shows Timon, a fabulously rich and self-destructively generous Athenian, in prosperity, the second in adversity. In the first part he is contrasted with the cynic philosopher Apemantus. The turning point comes when Timon learns that he has spent or given away all he owned and his flatterers are revealed, in skilfully satirical episodes that bear the stamp of Middleton's authorship, to be 'a knot of mouth-friends' (3.6.89), helping to justify Apemantus' cynicism.

In a bitter soliloquy Timon, tearing off his clothes, curses Athens and leaves for a cave in the woods:

> Nothing I'll bear from thee
> But nakedness, thou detestable town. (4.132–3)

The play's second part is virtually an interrupted soliloquy by Timon in which he encounters again the men he had known in his former way of life. The reversal in his fortunes has turned him into a bitter misanthrope. Now he resembles Apemantus, as a brilliant slanging match (4.3) between them shows, but Apemantus is a contented cynic whereas Timon needs to give full

emotional vent to his bitter rejection of mankind. The appearance
of his faithful steward Flavius comes as a reminder of the
possibility of love, loyalty, and friendship, and Timon comes to
accept, with difficulty, that he is mistaken in his wholesale
denunciation of mankind:

> I do proclaim
> One honest man—mistake me not, but one,
> No more, I pray—and he's a steward. (4.3.497–9)

The logical outcome of Timon's withdrawal from the human race
is a further retreat into the refuge of death: only extinction can
bring him what he desires:

> My long sickness
> Of health and living now begins to mend,
> And nothing brings me all things. (5.2.71–3)

And a strange but beautiful otherworldliness enters his speech as
he declares:

> Timon hath made his everlasting mansion
> Upon the beachèd verge of the salt flood,
> Who once a day with his embossèd froth
> The turbulent surge shall cover. (5.2.100–3)

The closing scenes are sketchy, but in the hands of a great actor
and with skilful textual tinkering the play can grow beyond satire
to tragedy.

Shakespeare drew far more extensively on Plutarch for his two last
classical plays, *Coriolanus* and *Antony and Cleopatra*, often
incorporating his ideas and even his language into their dialogue.
These plays form such sharply contrasting masterpieces that they
might be thought of as self-conscious attempts both to stretch his
imaginative faculties and to demonstrate his versatility. They show

Plutarch to have been a kindred spirit in their fascination with the idiosyncrasies and oddities of human psychology, and with the way that such characteristics can shape national as well as human destinies.

Coriolanus tells a story of war and peace, love and hate, division within a nation and within a family. Its broad framework of national warfare is epitomized in personal conflict between the Roman Caius Martius, who earns the honorific title of Coriolanus—conqueror of the city of Corioles—and Tullus Aufidius, leader of the Volsces. Their relationship, which has strongly homoerotic overtones, is ambiguous. After Coriolanus is banished from Rome Aufidius welcomes him with 'I . . . do contest'

> As hotly and as nobly with thy love
> As ever in ambitious strength I did
> Contend against thy valour. (4.5.109–13)

Within Rome, too, strife resolves itself into a largely personal conflict, between Coriolanus and the two unscrupulous Tribunes. His arrogance, inseparable from his valour, brings about his banishment so that from being the enemy within the state he becomes identified with the enemy outside it. And he is in conflict within his own family. His mother Volumnia, eager for his fame, expresses her love for him in paradoxical terms: 'O, he is wounded, I thank the gods for't' (3.1.114). Like him she hates the common people, but she advises him to dissemble with his nature to catch their votes, thus forcing a conflict within him: his efforts to perform the role she casts him in are ludicrous, but the issues of personal integrity and honour that lie at the heart of the play are focused in his ultimate refusal to do so,

> Lest I surcease to honour mine own truth,
> And by my body's action teach my mind
> A most inherent baseness. (3.2.121–3)

After he is banished he has to pretend to hate those he loves. But when his family—mother, wife, and son—enter the enemy camp to plead with him, he is forced into self-recognition: 'I melt, and am not | Of stronger earth than others' (5.3.28–9). His mother insists on the need for compromise; if he conquers Rome, he conquers her. The turning point comes wordlessly as, in a famous stage direction, he 'holds her by the hand, silent'. Acknowledging that he can no longer maintain a godlike aloofness from natural emotion, he accepts both the full burden of his humanity and the inevitability of his death.

The events of *Antony and Cleopatra* form a late sequel to those of *Julius Caesar*, but as usual Shakespeare manipulates history for dramatic effect. Antony has become an older man, though Octavius is still 'scarce-bearded'. The geographical scope of the play is much greater. Its characters move often and easily between Egypt and Rome. Empires are at stake; the play is peopled by their leaders. And the poetic and dramaturgical style is very different from that of the earlier play. Its poetry is predominantly supple, relaxed, and sensuous. Cleopatra's 'infinite variety' is created largely by the flexibility and range of the language that Shakespeare gives her to speak. Subtlety of characterization and sudden shifts of mood and tone fleck the dialogue with comedy.

Yet much of the action is domestic. Many scenes portray the home life of Egypt's queen. Often Shakespeare writes supremely theatrical, nuanced dialogue, breaking the bounds of the blank verse line, colloquial rather than overtly rhetorical in expression, giving great significance to oblique statements, exclamations, pauses, and silences, relying on his actors to fill the gaps with meaningful bodily movement, facial expressions, vocal nuance, and silent interaction. So when Cleopatra is brought to comfort Antony after his 'doting' withdrawal from battle:

| EROS | Nay, gentle madam, to him! Comfort him. |
| IRAS | Do, most dear Queen. |

CHARMIAN	Do? Why, what else?
CLEOPATRA	Let me sit down. O Juno!
ANTONY	No, no, no, no, no.
EROS	See you here, sir?
ANTONY	O, fie, fie, fie!
CHARMIAN	Madam.
IRAS	Madam, O good Empress!
EROS	Sir, sir! (3.9.25–34)

But when necessary Shakespeare rises to the height of poetic
eloquence. Like *Romeo and Juliet* this is a double tragedy, but here
the lovers die separately. A lot has to happen after Antony dies.
Shakespeare avoids the danger of anti-climax partly by introducing
a new character, the enigmatic rustic who brings Cleopatra the
instrument of her death, partly by the richly symbolic nature of her
conversation with him, but above all by creating the transcendent
though still richly characterful poetry of Cleopatra's closing speeches.

> Give me my robe. Put on my crown. I have
> Immortal longings in me. Now no more
> The juice of Egypt's grape shall moist this lip.

And, a few moments later, with a poignant touch of domesticity:

> Peace, peace!
> Dost thou not see the baby at my breast?

She dies (like Hotspur)—in mid-sentence:

> What should I stay—

And Charmian finishes her sentence for her:

> In this vile world.

Her infinite variety sustains her to the end; no other tragic
character dies so subtly nuanced a death.

Chapter 8
Tragicomedy

Shakespeare's restlessly imaginative exploration of the possibilities of comic form led him into new paths in four plays based on romance literature which, though they form the most closely interrelated group in all his output, nevertheless show him continuing to experiment with new dramatic techniques. All their plots include highly improbable and supernatural elements. All tell of high-born families and lovers separated by catastrophe, sometimes natural, at other times humanly contrived. All span large areas of space and time and involve leading characters in suffering.

In these plays the presentation of character tends rather to the general and the ideal than to psychological realism. Suffering is overcome, obstacles to reunion and reconciliation are removed, sometimes as the result of supernatural intervention, and harmony is restored. These characteristics, sometimes described as 'autumnal', resemble those in the late work of other artists, such as Rembrandt, Beethoven, Richard Strauss, and W. B. Yeats—but there is no reason to suppose that Shakespeare knew he was coming to the end of his career as he wrote them.

Pericles, based on the story used in the framework tale of *The Comedy of Errors* and exceptionally popular in its time—Jonson enviously called it a 'mouldy tale'—is a problematic work, uneven in style, textually corrupt in the surviving text printed in 1609 (which is probably why it was not included in the First Folio), written in part by George Wilkins (see Chapter 2), and (like *Timon of Athens*) badly in need of textual reconstruction if it is to be performed. (The Oxford edition offers such a reconstruction.) Exceptionally the play has a narrator, John Gower, a contemporary of Chaucer who had told the story in his poem *Confessio Amantis* (1385–93).

The earlier stages of the action, in which Pericles gains a wife, Thaisa, are episodic and garbled, but with the birth at sea of their daughter Marina followed by Thaisa's apparent death the play comes into focus. Marina is a mystically ideal portrayal of the power of chastity; her presence in a brothel whose inmates are sketched with a truly Shakespearian immediacy is one aspect of the play's use of extremes. As in all these plays we have a sense that life is controlled by inscrutable but ultimately beneficent powers symbolized by sea and tempest. Marina laments,

> Ay me, poor maid,
> Born in a tempest when my mother died,
> This world to me is but a ceaseless storm
> Whirring me from my friends. (15.69–72)

Out of the tempest comes a calm, aptly symbolized by music. Thaisa, believed dead and committed to the waves, is revived to the sound of instruments, and Marina sings to her father to try to restore him from his grief-induced coma. Their protracted but masterfully controlled reunion scene draws from Pericles lines that express recurrent ideas of these plays: the close relationship between the apparent extremes of pain and joy, and the capacity of young people to renew their parents' lives:

> O Helicanus, strike me, honoured sir,
> Give me a gash, put me to present pain,
> Lest this great sea of joys rushing upon me

O'erbear the shores of my mortality
And drown me with their sweetness!

Then he addresses his daughter:

> O, come hither,
> Thou that begett'st him that did thee beget,
> Thou that wast born at sea, buried at Tarsus,
> And found at sea again! (Scene 21.178–85)

When Marina's identity is established the music of the spheres induces in Pericles a vision of the goddess Diana leading to the revelation that his wife is alive and to the miraculously joyful outcome of the action.

The conjunction of extremes is even more apparent in *Cymbeline*, an absurdist fantasy which draws on both the historian Holinshed and the romance writer Boccaccio. Roman Britain and Renaissance Italy are improbably yoked together, and the play is peopled by antithetical characters. Some—Innogen, Pisanio, Belarius, and the children of nature Arviragus and Guiderius—are paragons of virtue; others, such as Cloten and his mother the Queen, 'Too bad for bad report' (1.1.17). Giacomo, who tricks Posthumus into believing that his wife Innogen is unfaithful, switches from outright villainy to implausible penitence; Posthumus from virtue to debasement brought about by Giacomo's deception and back to virtue again. Some put on a false front: the Queen conceals her villainy from most of those around her, and Posthumus is tricked into believing that Innogen is false to him. Some—Innogen, Cloten, Posthumus—are disguised for part of the action; others—Arviragus and Guiderius—don't know who they really are.

The language is often antithetical too, and the play reaches a grotesque climax of absurdity when Innogen wakes beside Cloten's headless corpse believing it to be that of her husband; her subsequent speech is perhaps the most bizarre and daring in the whole of Shakespeare.

> A headless man? The garments of Posthumus?
> I know the shape of 's leg; this is his hand,
> His foot Mercurial, his Martial thigh,
> The brawns of Hercules; but his Jovial face—
> Murder in heaven! How? 'Tis gone. (4.2.310–14)

Improbability flowers into magic as the god Jupiter appears to the sleeping Posthumus in a vision; in a long closing scene famous for an apparently endless series of revelations all disguises are removed, all identities made known, all misunderstandings removed. It is a virtuoso display of dramatic craftsmanship in which Shakespeare challenges his audiences to abandon all expectation of plausibility in favour of the glory of miracles achieved.

A miracle forms the climax of *The Winter's Tale*, based on Robert Greene's short novel *Pandosto, The Triumph of Time*, of 1588. The story moves in a manner typical of pastoral literature from the Sicilian court to the Bohemian countryside and back over a period of sixteen years. Leontes, King of Sicily, falsely believing that his wife's pregnancy is the result of an adulterous affair with Polixenes, King of Bohemia, passes through extremes of emotion from the near-tragedy of suffering caused by the death, for which he is responsible, of his son, and the apparent deaths of his wife Hermione and daughter Perdita—the name means 'the lost one'—through the 'saint-like sorrow' (5.1.2) of his penitence to the rapture of his final reunion with those he had believed dead.

Shakespeare picks up Greene's subtitle by giving Time a prominent place in his play's structure of ideas. His opening scene includes a poetic evocation of childish illusions of timelessness (1.1.63–77); Time makes a personal appearance as the Chorus (4.1); a speech by the young hero Florizel magically suggests that the beauty of Perdita and his love for her can suspend the passage of time (4.4.135–43); the concluding episodes show that time can offer opportunities for repentance and redemption; and a sense of renewal is created by the fact that the son and daughter of the estranged kings bring about their parents' reconciliation by their marriage.

The play's structure of ideas also includes the antithesis, common in the period, between art and nature, discussed in an unusually abstract passage of verse in 4.4, and a kind of art is apparent in the exercise of the will by which Leontes expresses penitence and the lovers control their ardour.

These ideas merge in the final scene. Shakespeare departs from his source in keeping Hermione alive, and the theatrically daring (and difficult) stroke of making her pose as her own statue is symbolically appropriate as well as a theatrical masterstroke. Her resurrection is a conquest over time. Self-control brings its rewards as art melts into nature and the stone becomes flesh. The play ends in the joy and wonder characteristic of romance literature, but they are counterpointed by our consciousness of the suffering out of which the miracle has emerged.

Whereas *Pericles*, *Cymbeline*, and *The Winter's Tale* take place over large tracts of space and time, in his last solo-authored play Shakespeare returns to the neo-classical limits of space and time that he had previously employed only in *The Comedy of Errors*: the action of *The Tempest* takes place in a single location and over a period of only a few hours. Though he drew heavily on his reading of travel literature, Ovid (quoted almost verbatim in Prospero's speech beginning 'Ye elves of hills, brooks, standing lakes and groves', 5.1.33–57), and John Florio's translation of Montaigne's essays, he invented the plot, creating his most overtly symbolical drama.

We see only the end of the story of Duke Prospero's expulsion with his baby daughter Miranda from Naples to a desert island, learning of its earlier stages in his long narration which sends Miranda to sleep (and has been known to have the same effect on audiences). Like Oberon in *A Midsummer Night's Dream*, the Duke in *Measure for Measure*, and Iago in *Othello*, Prospero is a playwright within the play, controlling its action as it takes place. Seeking to discipline his shipwrecked opponents, he needs self-discipline to do so. His power is magical but limited. He and his spirit helper Ariel can call up a masque for the entertainment and instruction of his daughter and her betrothed, Ferdinand, but it is 'such stuff | As dreams are made on', and vanishes 'into air, into thin air' as he remembers the 'foul conspiracy' on his life hatched by the island's only native inhabitant, Caliban (4.1.148–58). He can exercise moral influence but only on those who are predisposed to receive it. He himself has to learn from Ariel how to behave with full humanity (5.1.17–30).

It is easy to see *The Tempest* is an allegory of the artist—of Shakespeare himself—and his work. It relates also to many concepts that recur in Shakespeare's plays: art and nature; nature and fortune; justice and mercy; sin and retribution; guilt and repentance; illusion and reality; self-deception and self-knowledge. It is a supremely poetic drama, not just because it contains some of Shakespeare's greatest poetry but because it speaks, as the greatest poetry does, on many levels at once, universally relevant and—if we can hear Ariel's music—universally effective.

Shakespeare and Fletcher

It looks as if Shakespeare found John Fletcher a congenial colleague. At the very end of his career they worked together on three plays, one of which, *Cardenio*, has not survived. Traces of it may remain in a play of 1728 called *Double Falsehood, or The Distressed Lovers*, by Louis Theobald, which he said was based on one 'originally written by Shakespeare'.

The compilers of the First Folio, wishing to impose a degree of uniformity on the plays based on English history, gave the title of (in full) *The Famous History of the Life of King Henry the Eight* to the play about that king's reign which had been performed in 1613 as *All Is True*. It is a spectacular drama with many overtly theatrical set pieces, composed almost entirely in verse, and requires an unusually large cast. The action, covering the first part of Henry's reign, depicts Cardinal Wolsey's increasing abuse of his power, the execution, brought about by Wolsey, of the Duke of Buckingham, the King's abandonment of Queen Katherine (of Aragon), her trial and eventual death, the rise to favour of Anne Boleyn, Wolsey's disgrace, and the birth to Henry and Anne of a daughter instead of the hoped-for son.

King James I had been on the throne for a decade when this play appeared. Its climax is Archbishop Cranmer's baptism of the infant Queen Elizabeth I in a speech of prophecy which—rather like the closing speech of *Richard III*, spoken by Henry VIII's father—extends the time scheme beyond the events portrayed, through the intervening years, and up to the time of the play's first performance by looking forward to the peace and prosperity that, Cranmer predicts, England will enjoy as a consequence of the baby's birth. Although Cranmer declares that none should think his words 'flattery, for they'll find 'em truth', his speech is more likely to sound like a sycophantic eulogy not only of the dead Queen but of her successor James I, patron of the company who performed it. I like to think it was written by Fletcher rather than by Shakespeare.

The other surviving Fletcher collaboration, *The Two Noble Kinsmen*, not printed in the Folio, first appeared in 1634 as having been written 'by the memorable worthies of their time, Master John Fletcher and Master William Shakespeare'. A tragicomedy of the kind that became popular towards the end of the first decade of the 17th century, it is based on Chaucer's *Knight's Tale*, which Shakespeare had already drawn on for *A Midsummer Night's*

Dream. It dramatizes a romantic tale of the conflicting claims of love and friendship. Palamon and Arcite are the closest of friends—'Is there record of any two that loved better than we do, Arcite?' asks Palamon, 'I do not think it possible our friendship | Shall ever leave us' (2.2112–15)—but at that very moment Emilia, sister-in-law of Theseus, Duke of Athens, appears, and the men instantly become rivals for her love. Their conflict is finally resolved by a formal combat with Emilia as the prize, in which the loser is to be executed. Arcite wins, and Palamon's head is on the block when news arrives that Arcite has been thrown from his horse. Dying, he commends Emilia to his friend, and Theseus rounds the play off with a meditation on the paradoxes of fortune.

It is much easier in this play than in *All is True* to identify which dramatist wrote which episodes. Fletcher seems to have been mainly responsible for the amusing subplot telling of the love of a jailer's daughter for Palamon, and for the entertainment put on by rustics for the Duke, as in *A Midsummer Night's Dream*. Shakespeare's hand is more apparent in the rhetorically and ritualistically impressive Act 1 and for other episodes including most of Act 5. By this time his verse style has become rarefied and involuted, making no concessions to either actor or audience. At times it seems almost as if, like Beethoven in his late string quartets or Henry James in his late novels, he is writing for himself rather than for an audience. Can it be that he has lost the taste for overt theatricality, and that his colleagues encouraged him to work with a colleague who was more attuned to popular taste? Might one even dare to suggest the possibility that he gave up playwriting because, to put it crudely, he got the sack?

Epilogue

The plays and poems that I have described in this book have had, and continue increasingly to have, a major impact on many areas of human life. Fellow poets from Ben Jonson onwards have written appreciatively of Shakespeare and have been inspired by him both in their verse and in other writings. In the late 17th century the poet John Dryden adapted several of the plays to suit the taste of his time and wrote eloquently on Shakespeare's style. In the 18th century the poet Alexander Pope and the writer and lexicographer Samuel Johnson were among those who edited the complete plays, and the prefaces to their editions are classics of criticism.

The plays decreased in popularity during the late 17th and early 18th centuries, largely because of their violation of neo-classical principles of dramatic construction and the perceived impurities of their style. Some fell out of the repertoire, others were substantially rewritten. Sometimes adaptation was designed to take account of changed theatrical conditions, such as the introduction of female actors instead of boys, and the development of new staging methods such as the introduction of spectacular scenic effects. Sometimes it reflected new artistic criteria: Nahum Tate's 1681 version of *King Lear*, which enjoyed enormous popularity for well over a century, shortened and sentimentalized the play, giving it a happy ending and introducing a love interest between Edgar and Cordelia. Some adaptations changed plots to reflect contemporary political concerns.

A change came with the Jubilee of 1769, a festival held in Stratford-upon-Avon and directed by the great actor David Garrick who, in a celebratory ode, described Shakespeare as 'the god of my idolatry'. In spite of this he too acted in heavily adapted versions, many of which he prepared himself; some of them supplanted the original texts in the British and American theatre until well into the 19th century.

The plays began to be translated and adapted into European languages in the late 18th century, and both in Britain and overseas interest escalated during the Romantic period. Some of the most perceptive of all comments on Shakespeare come in John Keats's letters. Samuel Taylor Coleridge's and William Hazlitt's lectures and other writings are seminal works of Shakespeare criticism.

Over the years, philosophers and thinkers of many nationalities such as Voltaire (who wrote caustically about Shakespeare's violation of neo-classical artistic principles), Johann Wolfgang Goethe, Thomas Carlyle, John Ruskin, Georg Hegel, Karl Marx, Sigmund Freud, and Jacques Derrida have come under Shakespeare's influence and written about him. His works have been a continuing source of inspiration for creative writers. Jane Austen knew the plays well; Charles Dickens was soaked in Shakespeare: the plays feature prominently in the narratives of *Great Expectations* and in *Nicholas Nickleby*, and echoes, allusions, and quotations recur throughout his work. Herman Melville's *Moby Dick* (1851) evokes especially *King Lear*, and in his story *Billy Budd* (on which Britten based a great opera) the character of Claggart is indebted to Iago. *King Lear* lies behind Turgenev's *A King Lear of the Steppes*. Victor Hugo started to write an introduction to French translations of the plays written by his son, François-Victor, but it turned into a full-length book, mostly about himself. Oscar Wilde's *Portrait of Mr W.H.* is a prose fantasy based on the Sonnets and W. S. Gilbert wrote a hilarious skit on *Hamlet* called *Rosencrantz and Guildenstern*.

Hamlet also figures prominently in James Joyce's *Ulysses*, and Tom Stoppard's *Rosencrantz and Guildenstern are Dead* is another of the many offshoots of the play. Virginia Woolf wrote appreciatively of Shakespeare in essays and brings him before us in her fantasy novel *Orlando*. W. H. Auden's *The Sea and the Mirror* is a poetic fantasy based on *The Tempest*, and he delivered and published perceptive lectures on Shakespeare. Ted Hughes's *Shakespeare and the Goddess of Complete Being* is a densely written mythical study, and he also compiled an anthology of Shakespeare's verse. The Argentinian Jorge Luis Borges wrote movingly on Shakespeare's imagination. Edward Bond's *Lear* is a harsh offshoot of Shakespeare's tragedy and Bond's play *Bingo* portrays a suicidal Shakespeare's last days. *A Midsummer Night's Dream* figures prominently in Angela Carter's novel *Wise Children*, Jane Smiley reworks *King Lear* in modern terms in her novel *A Thousand Acres*, and John Updike's *Gertrude and Claudius* is a kind of prequel to *Hamlet*.

In music, the plays have inspired great operas such as Giuseppe Verdi's *Macbeth*, *Otello*, and *Falstaff*, Benjamin Britten's *A Midsummer Night's Dream*, Thomas Adès's *The Tempest*, Felix Mendelssohn's incidental music for *A Midsummer Night's Dream* with its universally known Wedding March, orchestral works such as Hector Berlioz's *Roméo et Juliette* and Pyotr Tchaikovsky's concert overture based on the same play, musicals such as Cole Porter's *Kiss me, Kate* and Leonard Bernstein's *West Side Story*, songs by Franz Schubert and Richard Strauss and Ralph Vaughan Williams and Johnny Dankworth, film music by William Walton and Dimitri Shostakovich, and ballet scores such as Serge Prokofiev's for *Romeo and Juliet*.

Starting around the middle of the 19th century in both Britain and America Shakespeare has become a major instrument of education for students of all ages, from primary school to graduate level and beyond. Increasingly this has become an international phenomenon. It has been reported, for example, that each year some 21,000,000 Chinese schoolchildren are required to read at least the trial scene from *The Merchant of Venice*.

All this educational activity has resulted in an enormous proliferation of publications including editions and handbooks designed for a wide variety of educational markets. It has not always achieved its objectives. In spite of efforts to enhance teaching methods it is not uncommon to hear people say that they were put off Shakespeare at school. In recent years the plays have been re-presented for a popular market in, for example, comic strip form and in manga versions, and allusions to them occur frequently in various kinds of popular entertainment including pop songs, television shows, and crossword puzzles.

Above all, Shakespeare's plays have been propagated through the medium for which they were written, theatrical performance, and in more recent times on film, radio, and television. Styles of performance have varied enormously, and politicizations of Shakespeare continue to the present day both in Britain and overseas, as for example in Richard Eyre's National Theatre 1990 production of *Richard III*, starring Ian McKellen and later adapted into a film by Richard Loncraine, in which the King inescapably recalled Hitler.

Not everyone approves of such versions. It is not uncommon to hear demands for 'straight' performance, in which the text is relatively unaltered and perhaps played in Elizabethan costume. But there are arguments against this. Total authenticity is unattainable, even were it desirable. Inevitably modern audiences bring preconceptions to the plays. If only for practical reasons, very few productions give complete texts even of the shorter plays. Increasingly it has become common to update them, often by dressing the actors in costumes of later periods, including the present, and putting a new perspective on the text by, for instance, the use of symbolic, interpretative devices and properties. Ralph Fiennes's film of *Coriolanus* transfers the action to the war zones of Serbia. *Hamlet* has proved particularly susceptible to such reinterpretation: rather as Ian McKellen's Richard III recalled Hitler, so a Romanian production of *Hamlet* introduced heavily political resonances—and affected interpretative response—by causing Gertrude and Claudius to resemble the dictator Ceausescu and his wife. Numerous other productions, especially of the tragedies, have used them for political purposes and for the expression of dissent from totalitarian regimes. Even a single phrase from one of Shakespeare's sonnets, 'art made tongue-tied by authority' (66), became a rallying cry for central European protests against political censorship. Some productions virtually rewrite the plays, creating on the basis of the original texts what are essentially new works of art. Such versions demand to be judged by the degree of success with which they achieve their own kind of artistic integrity: there are times when it seems that the director is a kind of failed playwright who exploits the Shakespeare text in order to propagate his or her own ideas.

Shakespeare's increasingly global popularity means that the plays are performed in what Cassius in *Julius Caesar* calls 'states unborn' and 'accents' that were 'yet unknown' when they were first written. Translation creates new linguistic and ideological effects. It is not necessarily reductive. Great writers such as André Gide and Boris Pasternak have translated some of the plays. A good translator can create great verse and prose on the basis of what Shakespeare wrote, transmuting it into something different but not necessarily any the less fine. The German version of the complete works (1791–1833) prepared by August Wilhelm Schlegel and completed under the supervision of Ludwig Tieck has become a classic in its own right. And whereas for English-speaking audiences Shakespeare's language is archaic, translators will normally use the current form of their own language, with perhaps occasional heightening or deliberate use of archaism.

In spite of the growing appreciation of Shakespeare, dissenting voices have been heard from time to time. Late in the 19th century the Russian novelist Leo Tolstoy declared manfully that he had repeatedly read the plays in Russian, German, and English 'with repulsion, weariness, and bewilderment' and launched a virulent attack on *King Lear*, claiming that the largely forgotten old play of *King Leir* was 'incomparably and in every respect superior to Shakespeare's adaptation'. And at around the same time Bernard Shaw—whose political principles resembled Tolstoy's—wrote with obvious and self-conscious irony,

> there is no eminent writer, not even Sir Walter Scott, whom I can despise so entirely as I despise Shakespear when I measure my mind against his. The intensity of my impatience with him occasionally reaches such a pitch, that it would positively be a relief to me to dig him up and throw stones at him, knowing as I do how incapable he and his worshippers are of understanding any less obvious form of indignity.

But Shaw followed this diatribe with one of the most eloquent (though still characteristically ironic) of all tributes to Shakespeare's greatness:

> I am bound to add that I pity the man who cannot enjoy Shakespear. He has outlasted thousands of abler thinkers, and will outlast a thousand more. His gift of telling a story (provided someone else told it to him first); his enormous power over language, as conspicuous in his senseless and silly abuse of it as in his miracles of expression; his humour; his sense of idiosyncratic character; and his prodigious fund of that vital energy, which is, it seems, the true differentiating property behind the faculties, good, bad, or indifferent, of the man of genius, enable him to entertain us so effectively that the imaginary scenes and people he has created become more real to us than our actual life—at least, until our knowledge and grip of actual life begins to deepen and glow beyond the common.

Increasingly it is becoming difficult to avoid Shakespeare, however hard one may try. Shakespeare festivals abound in many countries of the world—in Stratford-upon-Avon in England and in Stratford, Ontario, in Canada; in Central Park, New York, and Ashland, Oregon, to name only two of the numerous American Shakespeare festivals; in Romania at Craiova, in Hungary at Gyula, in Poland at Gdansk, in Germany at Neuss and Bremen. In Argentina and Brazil and Mexico and China and Japan and Australia, theatre festivals centre on Shakespeare or at least offer some of his plays. And in 2013 Shakespeare's Globe in London announced that it intended to tour a version of *Hamlet* to every country in the world—205 of them at the last count.

Shakespeare can be appreciated and enjoyed in many different ways. The most obvious way to get to know him is to see his plays performed in the medium for which he wrote them, the theatre. To do so is to experience simultaneously the art of the playwright and the art of his interpreters. The texts published in his lifetime and shortly afterwards are incomplete in themselves. He was a practical man of the theatre who knew that his actors would bring his words to life and in doing so would add to them a new dimension deriving from their own personalities and skills. A theatrical performance is a fusion of the text that the actors speak and the physical and emotional qualities of the actors who speak them. One reason for Shakespeare's continuing popularity is that he provides an astonishing range of roles in which actors of varying talents and personalities can simultaneously demonstrate their art and illuminate the texts they perform. In doing so they will rely also on the skills of stage designers, theatre directors, composers, choreographers, and all the other artists who contribute to a theatrical performance.

Of course, they may not always succeed. Actors may not measure up to their roles, and directors may not always provide a context in which their interpreters can give of their best. But an inadequate or misguided performance does not destroy the text on which it is based. Shakespeare's was a literary as well as a theatrical art. He was writing at a time in which, more than any other period in British theatrical history, the arts of literature and theatre went hand in hand. This means that although his plays reach full fruition only when they are acted, they also offer much to the reader, especially to a reader who can bring to them a theatrical imagination. Ideally the full appreciation of Shakespeare's plays results from the two-way process of reading them and seeing them performed.

In *Henry IV, Part Two*, Falstaff says, 'I am not only witty in myself, but the cause that wit is in other men' (1.2.9–10). This is true of Shakespeare too. His writings permeate the consciousness of mankind. They can stretch our imaginations, help us to understand ourselves, and touch our hearts. They speak of fundamental human instincts of ambition and desire, envy and hatred, friendship, compassion, and love. They can amuse us and they can move us to tears.

At the basis of all his work is a love of humanity. He knows to what heights it can reach. 'What a piece of work is a man!', says Hamlet. 'How noble in reason, how infinite in faculty, in form and moving how express and admirable, in action how like an angel, in apprehension how like a god—the beauty of the world, the paragon of animals!' (*Hamlet*, 2.2.305–9). Yet Shakespeare knows too that man is a 'quintessence of dust', and he creates the archetypal image of Hamlet, the prince of men, staring into the empty skull of Yorick, the dead jester. And King Lear speaks for everyone who has ever grieved over the death of someone they love when, over the dead body of his daughter Cordelia, he asks, 'Why should a dog, a horse, a rat have life, | And thou no breath at all?' (5.3.282–3).

Whether directly or indirectly, no one can remain untouched by Shakespeare. He is in the water supply; he is here to stay.

Shakespeare's works: a chronology

This table lists Shakespeare's works in a conjectural order of composition. A few of the works can be fairly precisely dated but for many of them we have only vague information, such as dates of publication which may have occurred long after composition, dates of performances which may not have been the first, or inclusion in Francis Meres's list (see Chapter 2) which tells us only that the plays listed there must have been written by 1598, when his book *Palladis Tamia* was published. The chronology of the early plays is particularly difficult to establish. This list is based on the 'Canon and Chronology' section in *William Shakespeare: A Textual Companion*, by Stanley Wells and Gary Taylor, with John Jowett and William Montgomery (Oxford, 1987).

The Two Gentlemen of Verona	1590–1
The Taming of the Shrew	1590–1
The First Part of the Contention (Henry VI, Part Two)	1591
Richard Duke of York (Henry VI, Part Three)	1591
Henry VI, Part One	1592
Titus Andronicus	1592
Richard III	1592–3
Venus and Adonis	1592–3
The Rape of Lucrece	1593–4
Edward III	1594
The Comedy of Errors	1594

Further reading

Editions

References in this book are to *Shakespeare: The Complete Works*, General Editors Stanley Wells and Gary Taylor; Oxford, OUP, 1986; 2nd edition, 2005.

Annotated editions of single works are available in the Oxford World's Classics series.

Reference

The New Cambridge Companion to Shakespeare, ed. Margreta de Grazia and Stanley Wells (Cambridge, CUP, 2010).
The Oxford Companion to Shakespeare, ed. Michael Dobson and Stanley Wells (Oxford, OUP, 2001).
Shakespeare: A Rough Guide, by Andrew Dickson (London, Penguin Books, 2005).

Life

T. W. Baldwin's *Shakspere's Smalle Latine and Less Greeke* was published in 1944 and is available online: <http://durer.press.illinois.edu/baldwin>

Recommended biographies of Shakespeare include Park Honan, *Shakespeare: A Life* (Oxford, OUP, 1998); Lois Potter, *The Life of William Shakespeare* (London, John Wiley, 2012).

Shakespeare by Bill Bryson (New York, Atlas Books, 2007) is a popular short life.

Life and Afterlife

Stanley Wells, *Shakespeare: For All Time* (London, Macmillan, 2002).

Gary Taylor, *Re-inventing Shakespeare* (New York, OUP, 1991): a lively and provocative history of cultural and critical responses to Shakespeare.

Sources

Robert S. Miola, *Shakespeare's Reading* (Oxford, OUP, 2000).
Kenneth Muir, *The Sources of Shakespeare's Plays* (London, Methuen, 1977).

Criticism

The Romantics on Shakespeare, ed. Jonathan Bate (London, Penguin, 1992): an anthology of responses to Shakespeare from some of the greatest critics and poets.

Edwin Wilson, ed., *Shaw on Shakespeare* (London, Cassell, 1961): some of the most provocatively witty and perceptive writing ever about Shakespeare.

Theatre

Jonathan Bate and Russell Jackson, eds., *Shakespeare: An Illustrated Stage History* (Oxford, OUP, 1996).
Andrew Gurr and Mariko Ichikawa, *Staging in Shakespeare's Theatres* (Oxford, OUP, 2000).
Peter Thomson, *Shakespeare's Theatre* (2nd edition, Cambridge, CUP, 1992).
Stanley Wells, ed., *Shakespeare in the Theatre: An Anthology of Criticism* (Oxford, OUP, 1997).
Stanley Wells, *Great Shakespeare Actors* (Oxford, OUP, 2015).

Film

Russell Jackson, *Shakespeare and English-Speaking Cinema* (Oxford, OUP, 2014).

Text

John Jowett, *Shakespeare and Text* (Oxford, OUP, 2007).

Authorship

Among books that can be recommended to anyone tempted to question who wrote Shakespeare are *Contested Will*, by James Shapiro (London, Faber and Faber, 2010); *Shakespeare Beyond Doubt*, ed. Paul Edmondson and Stanley Wells (Cambridge, CUP, 2013); Stanley Wells, *Why Shakespeare WAS Shakespeare* (Kindle, 2014). See also the Shakespeare Birthplace Trust website for a free e-book, *Shakespeare Bites Back*, by Paul Edmondson and Stanley Wells.

Language

David and Ben Crystal, *Shakespeare's Words* (London, Penguin, 2002): a comprehensive glossary and guide.

Russ McDonald, *Shakespeare and the Arts of Language* (Oxford, OUP, 2001).

Context

James Shapiro, *1599: A Year in the Life of William Shakespeare* (London, Faber and Faber, 2005).
Stanley Wells, *Shakespeare & Co.* (London, Penguin, 2006).

Index